SALLY SCHWEIZER has been an .... for nearly 40 years. She has a passionate and active interest in music, languages, gardening, handwork and the environment. Married to Christian and mother of four adult children, Sally has an abiding love for the treasures of childhood. She is the author of *Well, I Wonder, Childhood in the Modern World*.

By the same author:

Well, I Wonder, Childhood in the Modern World, A Handbook for Parents, Carers and Teachers

Under the Sky

Playing, Working and Enjoying Adventures in the Open Air

A Handbook for Parents, Carers and Teachers

Sally Schweizer

Sophia Books

For my husband Christian and children Lars, Mark, Sven and Nina

Sophia Books
Hillside House, The Square
Forest Row, East Sussex
RH18 5ES

www.rudolfsteinerpress.com

Published by Sophia Books 2009
An imprint of Rudolf Steiner Press

A catalogue record for this book is available from the British Library

ISBN 978 1 85584 215 1

Cover by Andrew Morgan Design featuring a photograph by Sally Schweizer
Typeset by DP Photosetting, Neath, West Glamorgan
Printed and bound in Malta by Gutenberg Press Ltd.

Mixed Sources
Product group from well-managed forests, and other controlled sources
www.fsc.org Cert no. TT-CoC-002424
© 1996 Forest Stewardship Council

The paper used for this book is FSC-certified and totally chlorine-free. FSC (the Forest Stewardship Council) is an international network to promote responsible management of the world's forests.

CONTENTS

Illustration Credits

All line drawings by Marije Rowling

Other kindergarten and outdoor photos by Christian and Sally Schweizer
All others from family archives: Lars, Mark, Sven and Nina Lange,
Neil Peacock, Hansjürg Lange, Roguey Doyle, Sebastian Welford,
Andrea Schweizer, Christian and Sally Schweizer.

My gratitude and love goes to everyone with whom I have shared activities and adventures under the sky: family and friends, my kindergarten assistants and students who braved wind and weather in our expeditions, the many trusting parents who saw me disappearing but returning with their lovely children. And those children themselves, most of whom thought under the sky was the only proper place to be.

The earth is your mother, she holds you,
The sky is your father, he protects you,
Sleep, sleep, sleep, sleep.
Rainbow is your sister, she loves you,
The winds are your brothers, they sing to you,
Sleep, sleep, sleep, sleep.
We are together always, we are together always,
There never was a time, when this was not so.

Native American lullaby

ACKNOWLEDGEMENTS

Heartfelt thanks to my husband for his patient help; to my children for inspiration, advice and help with photographs; to Sally Jenkinson, who supported and advised me; to Marije Rowling for transforming my sketches into beautiful illustrations; to my publisher Sevak Gulbekian and editors Eileen Lloyd and Matthew Barton; to my sister Roguey Doyle, my son Mark Lange, Rachel Jenkins, Janni Nicol and Mark Fielding for their particular support; and to kind parents, now-adult children, friends and family who allowed me to use photographs they or we took (for full photography credits, please see p. vi). I also warmly thank the following for their permission to use photographs.

Parents and teachers at St Michael's Steiner School kindergarten in Wandsworth, London for permission to use my photo taken in their tiny but excellent garden for the front cover; Andrea Schweizer and parents of Unterentfelden Kindergarten, Switzerland; the Royal Botanic Gardens, Kew at Wakehurst Place in Sussex; The National Trust at Standen and Sheffield Park Garden in Sussex; High Weald Furniture and Conservators of Ashdown Forest in Sussex; head teacher Elizabeth Pettersen and parents of Saltwood Primary School in Kent for pictures at Bowles Outdoor Activity Centre Week; head teacher Mrs Laurie-Ann Lamb, Graìnne and Philip Warner and parents of the Albemarle Primary School in Wimbledon, London; kindergarten teachers and parents at Michael Hall Steiner Waldorf School in Sussex, Hereford Steiner Academy, Rudolf Steiner School of South Devon, St Michael's Steiner School in Wandsworth, London; head teacher Anne Owens, teachers and parents at Ysgol y Foryd, head teacher Geoff Griffiths and parents at Cefn Mawr Primary School, head teacher Menna Young and parents at Ysgol Min y Ddôl, head teacher Richard Jones and parents at Ysgol Bodhyfryd in North Wales; and head teacher Philippa Thomas and parents at Comin Infants' School in Aberdare, Wales.

My thanks also to the late Clare Mullan for permission to use her poems.

I was unable to trace the authors of a few photos, but would be pleased to acknowledge them in a future edition. I have been unable to find the dates or

sources of some verses. I have made every effort to trace the owners of
copyrights; if I have infringed any, I offer my apologies and will gladly ask and
acknowledge them in future.

Cover Photo by Sally Schweizer with kind permission of Jennie and Martin
Glover, Natalie and Peter Larsen, Mihiri and Jin Yee Lim, Jo Simmonds and
staff of St Michael's Steiner Waldorf School, Wandsworth, London.

Back cover portrait by Lars Lange, *www.ltlphotography.co.uk*

FOREWORD

This marvellous handbook for parents, carers, teachers, and all those who feel concerned about the increasingly distant relationship children have with the natural world, provides the perfect antidote to the TV-bound lifestyle many children suffer today. Part diary, part explorer's log, part recipe for healthy and happy living, Sally Schweizer's book walks, runs and jumps its way through forests, gardens, seashores and 'Treasure Islands', rekindling that feeling of a child's unbounded joy in the amazing, messy, wet and wonderful world just outside the door. At a time when global changes call for adults to act ethically towards the planet, knowing and loving it intimately as a child, and getting immersed in it, must surely be the best preparation for acknowledging and accepting this responsibility in later years.

Sally explores the ways in which young children interact with their environment, how nature 'nurtures' them. She enters their world and understands the need little fingers have to explore, touch and investigate the world when it is new. Even gravel, she notes, so dull to an adult, is fascinating to a very young child! There is great appreciation for all aspects of the outdoor experience; rain is just another pleasure, like sunshine, but with other things to do in it. The changing seasons are reasons for delight and fun, and also care. Gardens are carefully dug and planted, and nourished with 'black gold' from the compost heap, with the promise of a rich yield. This encourages patience and perseverance in young gardeners and even a failed crop can provide a rich learning experience.

The sections on safety and designing outdoor spaces for children are full of invaluable information and practical advice. Children need movement and play for their overall development and sense of well-being, and here Sally provides an amazing array of imaginative ideas. Children savour the world in dugouts, dens, igloos, straw-bale houses, willow castles. They relish parties in a park or near a stream, taking night walks and telling stories in the dark, making scarecrows, playing traditional games such as Fox and Hen, Cat and Mouse, and creating theatres in which the outdoor landscape becomes the scenery and stage, with nature generously providing the props.

Music is not forgotten. The book is studded with outdoor songs for all eventualities. There are songs for fun, celebration and praise, and others for endurance and courage—for when a hike becomes a haul, or when darkness descends unexpectedly on a troop of explorers, and spirits need to be lifted.

This is an uplifting philosophy of childhood and life, and an absolute treasure-trove of information for anyone who believes nature and childhood are perfect companions. Sally manages to combine magic with common sense—no mean feat—in this wonderful book, which is authentic from cover to cover. What she writes with such lively enthusiasm she has also lived.

Sally Jenkinson

INTRODUCTION

A hundred years ago, the great child-educator and philosopher Margaret McMillan said, 'The best classroom and richest cupboard is roofed only by the sky.' I believe that children who connect creatively with the natural world can have a quality of life in which the need for material possessions seems to fade. Creating their own risk management, children learn to confront the unexpected. Allowing and enabling them to do so kindles their love, respect and responsibility for the natural world.

Millions of people are suffering from our misuse and over-exploitation of the planet, which also leads to poverty. Destruction of the environment continues through thoughtlessness and greed. Thankfully many are working to protect and restore the environment: to preserve what is left, save the world's oceans and bring about a balance between humanity's real needs and the natural world, thus also developing a longer-term view of our global future. Sustainable agriculture and forestry are increasingly put into practice around the planet.

The opposite of this—short-term thinking which responds only to immediate concerns and fails to put the planet's ultimate well-being above its exploitation—is something that a narrowly intellectual education can do little to redress. Emphasis on early formal learning before the child has basic developmental, cognitive and social preparation is, in my opinion, detrimental. Research into younger children's use of TV, computers and other media shows harmful effects on brain and soul. As I have highlighted in this book, movement plays a key role throughout children's development. Climbing a tree sets the brain moving in a dynamic, interactive way. Respect for the grandeur of nature is inspired by reaching the top of a hill or mountain; watching the moon waxing and waning opens soul and spirit to the wonders of life.

Growing food and getting hands dirty is a wonderful learning experience, and seeing hungry birds at a bird table can set children quivering with delight. Simple things, such as sowing seeds and watching them come up—only to see them wither and die, perhaps because they were not watered—is an experience not soon forgotten. Many older folks bemoan an excess of

'Elfansafety', which although protecting children to a certain degree also stifles play and hinders progress. People are rediscovering the importance of the outdoors in education. Imaginative outdoor playgrounds are reappearing here and abroad, equipped with tree stumps, bushes, logs, ropes, boulders and the like—proper places for children to play and exercise body and mind.

Personally, I have many memories of bliss connected with the outdoors and especially water. I spent much of my free time in childhood up trees, at ponds and on farms, getting wet and muddy. We had picnics and swam in the sea and rivers. As a young adult I hiked and skied my way through the Alps. I learned how to camp with a minimum of clutter, even with a folding canoe on a Vespa scooter with first husband; the canoe skin served as tent floor and ends, and a flysheet formed the roof! This all helped me later as a single parent when camping, hiking and biking with my children, for instance getting our small tent up in a storm or hanging onto the younger two along a windy mountain ridge. My family and I have always enjoyed outdoor times. A love of gardening and flowers was inspired by my mother and aunt. My father was

Lovely river mud

passionate about his vegetable garden, but also spent whatever time he could messing about on his large sailing boat in which we sometimes slept, waking to the sight of seals and water birds in the river. My uncles taught me the glories of walking and listening to the birds. After a long day at work, I have often spent an hour pottering in the garden without going indoors first, gathering my thoughts and renewing my strength amidst nature.

Forty-five years of bringing up my own children and helping to educate those of others have convinced me that children develop very well under the sky. Before formal learning for young children became the norm and electronic media took such a hold, children spent much longer out of doors in fresh air and natural light. Safety was a common-sense issue. Outdoors, the young can communicate with nature and each other and feel no one is looking over their shoulder. Less pressure outside means easier sociable cooperation and negotiation. Children learn to respect the environment and in turn each other, with time to play, understand, to *be*. Many educators recognize that working and playing beneath the sky is important to all learning, not just a nice thing to do on the odd school trip. The rising number of 'forest' or 'woodland' schools verifies this. Many schools now have a garden with pond, vegetables and animals. By experiencing lettuces growing in soil, children develop a direct relationship to the earth. Some city classes have regular visits to the countryside. Teachers find behaviour improving as children become constructively energetic. Some with communication difficulties feel freer, so develop better under the sky; shy children become more confident. It is often quieter outdoors, away from radio and TV, mobiles, sirens and otherwise inescapable, unwelcome sounds—a relief to many children. In woods and fields they are not faced with traffic or advertising and the pace is slower.

The beneficial effects of exercise outdoors for body and soul are generally recognized. A friend with a high-powered job said he felt better—refreshed and *different*—if he could be out even for 10 minutes. It is of great concern to me that so many children are denied joys and courage-building exercises outdoors. As I will describe in this book, I believe children need to be outside for every aspect of their development, not least their social interaction, the paucity of which is at the heart of many of the world's problems.

People are generally becoming more aware of the dangers of a top-heavy indoor existence with little movement, and the problems related to screen addiction. Some parents walk with their children if they can, realizing this time is a gift for exercise, thoughtful moments and conversation. Children take their lead from us; if we show pleasure in the outdoors, even in rain and windy weather, they will too. I hope this book will prove useful to anyone who lives or works with children, and that it will encourage readers to have a go at extending education beyond the confines of the head and the four walls into the living dynamic of nature. There is so much one can do with imagination, experimentation and ingenuity.

Nature in different countries, from dunes and fjords to autumn colours and rocky deserts, shows its vast gifts of diversity. But around the world today we find Mother Nature struggling. She needs cherishing through humanity's abstinence, sacrifice and wisdom—not easy when many of us are accustomed to being materially pampered. People also need cherishing in many parts of the world: the poor, homeless and hungry. But we should not forget, either, the impoverishment of children who have little outdoor experience, and who therefore lose their connection with a source of strength, joy and renewal. This book aims to play a small part in re-establishing that connection.

1 Joyous sunset

2 A place to play

3 Happy Elinor

4 Another place to play

5 Our kindergarten mosaic made by family, parents, staff and children

6 Doorway

7 Mosaic centre

8 Part of retaining wall

1

THE FIRST YEARS OF CHILDHOOD

Heaven

The sky is blue,
The birds are singing,
The trees are green,
The wood is ringing,
The air is fresh,
The pools are clear.

Heaven is here.

Clare Mullan, aged 8

Early consciousness

Wonder, love and imagination build up the riches of original thought and depth of empathy for one's fellow human beings and the world. Light streaming through trees brings joy to the child. Feelings of interest and awe kindle the qualities of curiosity and wonder, encouraging discovery and invention. Through contact with their surroundings, children gain a relationship to the world that nurtures and promotes early brain-development processes. They need to *revisit* places and activities to keep strengthening their sense of belonging and identity.

Tell me and I will forget.
Show me and I may remember.
Involve me and I will understand.

Confucius

In the younger child particularly, understanding comes about through involvement and discovery more readily than formal teaching. The young child experiences the world as a unity, in which subjects flow in and out of each other rather than being compartmentalized. Generally, as adults, we remember about 10 per cent of what we read, 20 per cent of what we hear, 30 per cent of what we see, but 80 per cent of what we do. The younger child's experience is absolutely bound up with hands-on experience.

Added to this universality in the child up to 7 or so is the phenomenon of immersing oneself in others or events. A sense of individual identity begins around 3 years when children realize they are not the same as everything else. Before then there is complete identity of the self with the world. For instance, a 2-year-old pointed to a child with hair clips: 'What's in her hair?'—'Hair clips. She's got two hair clips,' said her mother. Then her daughter pointed to herself and said, 'She's got two hair clips.' Typical here is the child referring to herself as 'she', without a sense of separate identity that the word 'I' denotes. At age 5, Millie held a doll. 'This is me when I was little—when I was a child.' An 8-year-old would hardly say it because by then children can see themselves as separate individuals. The round, unformed faces of young children, which may make it difficult to know their sex, is a picture of their unformed and completely impressionable consciousness, whereas by 6 or so the features become more defined.

Young children lap up their environment through body and senses rather than their thinking: touching objects and putting them into their mouths like puppies. Each impression permeates their whole being in actual, physical encounter. In shops, small fingers explore shelves, boxes, ribbons and jars, while feet squeeze into a corner or stand half under the clothes rack. 'Don't touch! Come away from there. Leave that alone!' we may say. But it helps if we understand that the child actually needs to touch in order to investigate and make a proper acquaintance with the violin, bradawl or other object we are nervous about. So instead we can help: 'You may draw the bow over the strings while I hold it for you.' Or: 'Let's make a hole together.' Only gradually do thought processes take hold. For example, Sophia, just 4, said, 'My head is so long I couldn't fit in a shoe box.' Flossy, 6, wondering and slightly unsure: 'She's too big to fit in a shoe box.'

Young children are interested in everything, and learn naturally and easily through daily living. We barely need to show or tell them anything. Their assimilation and accommodation processes enable them to copy and repeat their experience. Whatever moves has fascination for children because they live in movement themselves, as any parent knows. One day, when I was preparing a puppet play, parents encouraged their children to watch. Yet the children had already begun to wander towards me as they saw the figures moving about silently. Children who watch such a puppet show may well want to do it themselves afterwards. They imitate what they experience.

There is so much of interest to be seen close to home: funny-looking clouds, cracks in the road, Mr Dundle with his green hat, berries, hoarfrost in the tree, a street light not working, apple blossom. Once I watched a 2-year-old sitting open-mouthed in her buggy in the park, staring up at an enormous rhododendron bush full of enormous red flowers while her mother chatted to a friend. After a few minutes, the mother noticed the bush and said excitedly to her daughter, 'Look, oh look, Sophie, up there, all those pretty flowers. Aren't they pretty!' She bent a branch down to show Sophie, but her dreamy immersion and attention had now been distracted by her mother, so she looked elsewhere.

On another occasion I was delighted to see a mother pushing a buggy full of shopping while her 18-month-old trotted alongside. When I said how lovely that was, the little one stood still and stared at me. She continued staring there for a couple of minutes until I was out of sight, despite her mother's encouragements to come.

Many children's stories and poems invest such things as trees, tractors and animals with human characteristics, because younger children identify with everything around them in one, unified consciousness. The following poem is a favourite, especially when enlivened by running, dancing, hopping, hiding and sinking down. It must have been written by someone who understood what children are like.

> *The North Wind came along one day, so strong and full of fun,*
> *He called the leaves down from the trees and said, 'Run, children, run!'*
> *They came in red and yellow dress, in shaded green and brown,*
> *And all the short November day, he chased them round the town.*
> *They came in groups, they came alone, they hid behind the trees,*
> *And when he found them hiding there, he said, 'No stopping please!'*
> *But when he found them tired out, all huddled on the ground,*
> *He softly said, 'Good night, my dears, now let us go to sleep.*

Author unknown

A simple, undemanding environment

Since young children soak up whatever is around them, the healthier their environment the better this will be for their development. People naturally have different ideas and opinions about what is healthy. I believe in keeping simplicity at the core of young children's lives, both in material things and activities. Since they live in the moment, only slowly becoming able to look forward or back, too many impressions can be overwhelming and unsettling.

> Granny went to do 'exciting things' with 3-year-old Elinor while Daddy fetched Mummy from the airport. 'We took a little bucket and spade and went to the swings, then played in a sandy place. It was a total surprise when they returned because we had rather forgotten what we went for.'

Children are naturally inquisitive. 'Where are you going?—Why?—What are you doing?—What is that?—What's it for?—How do you put it on there?—Can I do it? They want to explore and discover and experiment with their hands and feet.

It seems to me that a really important part of the environment we offer is allowing children to have enough time and space to explore and investigate, including away from adults' eyes. Unsupervised play outdoors expands and hones every kind of skill and proficiency. I have known many challenging children who flourished and settled harmoniously when given enough time for unstructured play and enticing, exciting, child-appropriate, simple adventures. There is a freedom outdoors that is not so easily found inside. If surroundings are undemanding and conducive to adventure, children can be themselves, free from inhibitions. For example, autistic Gerald was destructive and influenced others negatively. Outside he became a different person, more concentrated, responsive and easier to approach.

> Time and again I have seen a positive effect on children who were fearful, unable to play, bullied or bullies. Behaviour patterns and groupings of children of all ages change out of doors. They often mix more and play with children with whom they did not play before.

Sometimes over 20 children played harmoniously together in and around our sandpit of roughly 15 square metres. Things are often quieter and calmer outdoors, allowing adults to find time and space to have a chat with a child. A 7-year-old came to help me when I was gardening in someone else's school. More children came to help. Then I said goodbye and thanked everyone. The 7-year-old followed me to the gate. I thanked her once more. She said,

'Thank you for letting me help you.' A simple environment of helping and respect for one another goes deep.

Another time, a tough little 7-year-old watched me making a dandelion crown, then said he wanted one. He collected dandelions and we made another. It is delightful to see children revelling in natural things. Once I moved a beetle off my skirt, whereupon it played dead, only coming to life when we put a piece of bread near it the size of itself. It spent 20 minutes devouring the entire piece. Being full, it walked slowly away ignoring an apple crumb for dessert. I am convinced that the more space we give to mystery, wonder and magic in childhood the more profound their scientific discovery and invention will be later. Enough time for exploration is essential. Children who live in the country are lucky in having the outdoors on their doorstep, yet nowadays many do not use it. A country playgroup leader said some children do not know how to dig a little hole. City children flourish in an unpressurized environment at a child's slower pace, with the chance to play outdoors.

Sensory experience

Children live through their senses. As the capacity for abstract thinking slowly develops, the senses become more secondary, but in childhood they are paramount. A rich and diverse sensory environment in childhood gives a foundation, later, for alert sensing of other people's feelings and thoughts. Thus sensory experience is also the basis of our engaged relationship with the world as adults.

Outdoors, children's senses find nourishment, the basis on which they later learn abstract theories and respond to the world: fruit, berries, herbs excite the taste; furry animals, red hot poker plants, golden grain fields and swirling water engage the eyes. The nose enjoys flower scents, muddy carrots and gardens after rain. Ears are touched by birdsong, wind in trees and running on gravel. Songs, games and stories experienced outside amongst birds, rustling leaves and creaking branches are unforgettable impressions. The young soul is enlivened by cold and heat in frost and sun, cool puddles or hot sand. Interest is awakened in touching wet and dry stones, frozen soil, prickles, rough bark and furry leaves. Equilibrium develops in walking over uneven logs, climbing, paddling, watching clear skies after a storm or experiencing sunrise and sunset. Excitement or much creative activity makes children hold their

Curiosity under the bridge

Ryan investigating

Elinor's fine look-out

breath or breathe faster, but afterwards they relax and calm down again. Don't we unwind differently outside? After a rainy walk, it is lovely to have dry clothes, a warm drink and song. Children are so open to their new world, absorbent as blotting paper yet only able to deal with a small amount of impressions at a time. They are also easily overwhelmed—like the little child who screamed at the loud, opening chords of a Beethoven symphony.

Moving in diverse ways, such as in digging, raking, whistling, steadying oneself on fallen logs, climbing or hauling on a rope, all strengthen a healthy sense of being active in the world. A sense of movement also arises in wind, swirling mist or even through watching flowing water. A feeling of well-being comes about in fun, excitement and adventure: sheltering from the rain in a bush, singing from the top of a tree, skipping, or going for a really long walk.

> 'Yes, dear, very nice, dear,' said a frustrated parent pulling her child's hand, wondering whether they would ever get home. But for the child this was the most breathtaking wonder of the whole shopping expedition, the magical little carpet of moss at the bottom of the drainpipe with its miniature forest of trees (spore capsules).

Rhythms, repetitions and change

Research has found that seeing the same advertisement repeated many times imprints itself (unfortunately) most deeply on the child's mind. But used wisely, repetition and rhythm have a profoundly positive effect.

There are many rhythms in nature, such as leaves fluttering, raindrops falling, tides flowing in and out, frogs croaking or even seeds rattling in their pods.

If children hear from adults that outside is dirty, prickly, cold, wet, too hot or full of nasty insects, then they may be fearful when faced with going there. Some who came to my kindergarten disliked going outside, yet soon found its attractions. Rhythm (repeated experience) rather than many new impressions is of the essence here. It is wise to keep to the same routine and rhythms, also when on expeditions with younger children. They find the repetitions comforting, which relieves them from the need to think or worry about what they have to do. They also begin to recognize familiar landmarks on the journey, thus strengthening their sense of place. The changing seasons also offer ancient, archetypal ways of marking time: the first snows, autumn conkers, long days with short nights for example.

Using the limbs in connection with repeated trips helps the development of coordination and nurtures memory. Our kindergarten routines outdoors were the same as indoors and entailed the repetition of seasonal songs and poems at the same point each morning; then having our break, when drink was poured first and the children served each other. Always the same order and regularity, which the adult may consider 'boring' but which gives the child deep security.

Likewise, all children benefit from the chance to experience opposites, as this strengthens their sense of inner equilibrium. Such varied events are easily found out of doors: for instance playing in water contrasted with building with rocks and logs; singing, contrasted with listening to birdsong; picking flowers then making mud cakes. Nature offers a multitude of balancing opposites, from a pale morning sky to a red sunset, or from a soft leaf to a prickly stem. In other words, we need the opposites—say of spring and autumn—to create a sense of wholeness in ourselves. We better appreciate the joys of spring and summer if we share in the dying of autumn and winter. The rich diversity of weather and the rhythms between rain and sun, wind and calm have an enlivening effect. And mud in small quantities after all is not dangerous!

'I'm much powerfuller than you,' a 5-year-old told me from his lookout in the tree.

One rainy expedition Tuesday, we were eating our kindergarten break outside. Julie had not been coming if it was wet, but today she did. I said, 'You used not to like the rain. And look at the big smile on your face now!' She grinned.

Liking rhythm and routine, though, children can also be bewildered by irregular or sudden changes, or too much choice.

A warm autumn sun shone on the little family as they sat down in the Tea Garden after a long walk. 'I wonder what we'll have,' said Mum. 'Samwidge, drink o' water, cake,' said her 5-year-old. 'Samwidge, drink o' water, cake; samwidge, drink o' water, cake,' he repeated. 'Cake,' repeated the 3-year-old. 'Samwidge, drink o' water, cake; samwidge, drink o' water, cake,' they both repeated in this inspired musical rhythm. The menu arrived. Mum asked, 'What sort of sandwiches shall we have? Cheese, tuna, beef, strawberry jam . . .' The children were silent, unable to choose from such a confusing range of options. Then: 'Samwidge, drink o' water, cake; samwidge, drink o' water, cake.'—'Yes, but which *sort?*' pressed Dad. Later the question came about the cake: 'Lemon, coffee, chocolate, fruit?' Again no answer; the children really needed their parents to choose.

Cultivating a work ethic, incentive and independence

What a blessing it is if children are busy, taking initiative, playing, rolling, jumping, skipping and exploring: happy, strong and fulfilled. Partly because younger children are naturally so busy in their body, I believe it is wise not to expose them to televisual media.

A boy of just 2 came down steep steps one at a time, holding the rail. His mother tried to take his hand but he waved it away firmly.

Luca, aged $2\frac{1}{2}$, was running, running, running after a pigeon on the town square. He didn't try to catch it but simply copied the movements of the bird (which was in turn trying to get away from the child). This continued for many tireless minutes.

Children under about 6 are often active in silence. A girl of 2 tugged at her grandmother's arm. 'Not that way, dear.' The child continued to pull silently but insistently until grandmother gave in.

Ryan, a slender 6-year-old who often helped his parents outside, carried a pair of heavy oak paddles down a long flight of steep steps to the river. 'Aren't they a bit heavy for you?' asked his grandfather. 'No, *I'm* heavy.' And another time he struggled to lock the horse's gate, finally managing by leaning on it. 'I had to use my body as a tool.'

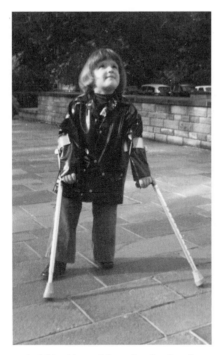

A child with special needs takes her first joyful steps

Children are independent already very early, nowhere more so than in their movement. Watching a baby struggling to hold his head up or repeatedly rolling over demonstrates this eagerness. In front of a screen, they are absorbed in a way unnatural to them because the images are moving but they themselves are not, so they become tired in mind rather than body, leading to frustration and dissatisfaction. Yet at the same time, the powerful lure of the screen is addictive. And adults come to depend on it to keep children quiet. The hostess of a beautiful ranch resort told me: 'Some guests are quite frantic when they realize that there is a television only in the day room; the children especially are in tears of desperation. Guests can walk enchanting trails but many go a little way then return to the day room.'

Young children often do seemingly nothing particularly constructive. The constructiveness lies, however, in the development and strengthening of their muscles, ligaments, respiration, circulation and other organs: in short, the body. This constitutes the best prerequisite for further soul maturity and prepares the child for the flowering of individual spirit in adulthood.

From the age of around 6, children begin to be more purposeful and directed in their activities. Originality and independence grow slowly from the imitative stage to that of planning without adult input. Children who can play together outdoors, create dugouts, build dens, re-enact stories and, in the best sense, muck about, are happy for days on end, while their ingenuity and perseverance blossom.

Respect, love and care in the natural world

The basis for much-needed ecological awareness in adulthood is a childhood spent in loving engagement and identification with the natural world in all its forms.

Loving care

Sven, 7, spent much time on holiday saving flies and bees from drowning with no fear of stings.

In a park, two small boys were feeding the ducks. 'Quack ... Quack, Quack, Quack ... Quack, Quack ... Quack, Quack, Quack ...' said the ducks. 'Are they singing, Granddad?' Granddad put his head on one side and listened. 'Yes, I suppose it's a sort of song.'

Every autumn we planted bulbs in kindergarten. We would make a fence of bent-over dogwood prunings to protect them from feet in spring, removing it again when the bulbs finished flowering. This work could last several days in short stints, quite tricky but the children enjoyed it. They felt an affinity and love towards the bulbs waking beneath the ground. But if taught by adult reactions that certain creatures are frightening or not nice, they may become cynical or afraid, and so squash worms, hurt cats and the like. For instance, Shelly's father would hold worms and spiders under his nose with horrid noises, giving him a lifelong fear of such creatures. Once some children discovered an ants' nest under a piece of bark, sending them scurrying about saving their eggs. One was fearful and wanted to squash

Fence for bulbs

them, but others admonished him. One child even *ate* them in handfuls, to
the horror of the others. Their teacher said, 'Let's put their roof back and
leave them in peace.' Not long after, curiosity overcame them and they
removed it. She said just the children who knew how to look after the ants
could stay there quietly and watch. But the child who ate them tried again.
The teacher told him it would soon be lunchtime and he wouldn't be able to
eat if he had a full tummy—and he stopped. At this age, a purely factual
instruction is more effective than moral indignation.

Seeing a Daddy-long-legs, Jimmy, who liked his food said, 'What do they
eat?' On finding a squashed worm on the road, a little group said, 'We'll
make him a grave', which they then decorated with daisies.

One of our children, aged 18 months, sat on top of a large anthill. The
ants crawled all over him but none bit him, although they did me. Was
this due to lack of fear? Young children are intuitively close to the
elemental world of nature. Some grown ups dismiss such things as fantasy,
or belittle 'fairies' by making silly, sentimental images of them. Yet since
time immemorial, poets, artists and musicians have depicted an elemental
world. I do believe there is more than material science to photosynthesis
and cell division in my garden.

Joy, harmony and originality

Meaningful work is imitated by young children, whilst older ones become more consciously active and look up to their elders. They like to organize each other and are responsible enough to see a job through.

> A boy of 7 watched me weeding a brick path. I asked if he wanted to help. 'No, I don't like getting my hands dirty.' Later he decided he would take the full wheelbarrow to the compost heap as his hands would stay clean and he liked pushing things about. Then he started to poke about between the bricks with a small fork. Gradually he began to pull the weeds out, and when it was time to go home a couple of happy hours later, I suggested he wash his by now very grubby hands. 'No, I like them dirty.'
>
> Having spent an hour outdoors, a 6-year-old said, 'We didn't have very *long* outside today.'

A postman told me that he loved his job and would never want to work inside. Rain and cold did not bother him as he carried the letters about. He found it sad that materialism has taken such a hold that many people do not appreciate the joys of the outdoor world. He said: 'Childhood has been trashed, swept from under their feet. We need to put a sense of community back into childhood, and let children come out of their houses to play together out of doors.'

Path weeding

A good outdoor space helps to create happiness and harmony. Children's innocence is well matched by the wonders of nature. They may stand back or go on a cheerful voyage of exploration. Helping to create or change part of a garden or playground is a golden opportunity for strengthening the body and creating a sense of purpose. Children may like to dig, pass bricks, set stones or plant trees.

Surprises delight children, like the frog hiding under old carpet in a pre-school garden, or a spider making its incredible, spiralling web. In fallen rose petals, a child may see fairy letters, fallen stars or goblins' plates. Pine cones on branches may appear to be a crowd of small people chatting. The natural world is music to children's ears, eyes and soul, inspiration to playfulness and invention. They enjoy reading a book perched high in a tree, and feel gloriously brave running into a patch of nettles, suffering in close-lipped, smiling agony afterwards. They like dug-up clay, go-carts, battered buckets, string, rabbits to feed. In my childhood, we found holes to flop into on the marshy riverbank, returning home covered in dried mud with the wind in our hair and singing at the tops of our voices.

I am convinced children learn to socialize better playing outdoors than in front of a TV or computer, without much adult interaction, and without being asked too many questions. In my experience, a mixed age group of children under 7 or 8 also fosters sociability. It is like a family. Many children today do not experience much family life, so such mixed age groups in an educational setting can compensate to some degree. Early years' centres and even schools can be like a home with a garden, where children can also learn to cook, clean, wash and grow vegetables—all security-building activities which they may not come across at home. Learning to take care of their environment instils a feeling of caring for each other. Older children like to help the younger, for instance to dress and undress, giving a sense of well-being and generosity to both. It is wonderful when staff really support each other too, especially when there are troubles between parents, for this shows an image of care between people and for the world. Where parents are separated, spending time outside with the children can be a relief in the neutral surroundings and lovable scenes of the natural world.

Hear, the evening bells are ringing, bells are ringing,
Far across the fields are sounding, fields are sounding,
Ding, dong, ding, dong.

Author unknown

In summary

Children are deeply connected with the world of nature. When their natural enthusiasm and inborn feeling of reverence are fostered in childhood, an inner strength and harmony develops in them, leading later to an inner freedom of thought and action in adulthood. The foundation for this sense of freedom and connection is to give the child opportunity for movement. The next chapter takes up this theme in more detail.

2
JOY IN MOVEMENT

Movement as the basis for all development

Sociability increases when children play together in a way that involves movement of body, heart and mind. Children need movement to develop the brain, which is inextricably linked with the body. Through practice of movement and balance, brain, body and mind become mobile and flexible. Sitting still requires a complex combination of muscles, so children need varied movement practice to exercise this control.

Watching young children play, one could wonder why they are given directed exercise. On kindergarten walks we passed a wall about 80 cm high, 20 cm wide and 50 m long. Every time, without invitation, nearly all of them

Togetherness in discovery

Self-initiated balance and sociability

Physical and social skills

scrambled up and balanced along it. They did not fall off. Children who have been allowed much free movement seem to know what they are capable of and come to no harm. When they come upon a polished floor, they may be inspired to use it as a slide. 80-year-old Heather could not walk her year-old dog enough any more, and found him a 'real pain'. Her son took him to live with them, so he enjoyed walks and played in the garden, becoming properly tired so all was well. Children are like that: if they are cooped up they can be a 'pain'. Dogs' and children's bodies need lots of exercise. Playing outside makes them hungry for a solid meal rather than a few snacks, and properly tired, ready for good sleep.

Three women were walking through the heath. A child of 4 ran on ahead, crawled through the heather, ran back and picked up stones in both hands, ran into the bushes and out again, walked with them for a few yards, then ran along with her legs out sideways, head and pigtails bobbing. This happy activity continued all the way. Young children don't much like walking in a straight line from A to B, but when their activity and imagination is engaged they love to follow its lead in all directions.

A 2-year-old ran anywhere but where her father was heading for. She ran to a bench, picked up some litter, ran round a tree and back to her father, then in the opposite direction, dropping the litter on the way. This continued until they reached the road. He wisely let her play, continuing walking but keeping an eye on where she was.

'Excuse me, do you have the time?' asked the mother of 7- and 3-year-olds in the woods. 'Gracious, we've been out two hours! They've had a fantastic time, climbing trees, digging trenches, running about.' An hour later we met again at the top of the hill. Her little one was grumpy now. 'He's tired. We're going home.' But how they had enjoyed those marvellous hours under the sky.

Young children are so light; they can roll about, jump up and fall without harm like a gymnast or dancer. They can't be still for long! Elinor, $2\frac{1}{2}$, confidently climbed very high on the climbing frame—to her grandfather's consternation. Even 4-year-olds can go on family bike rides. Children can walk quite far as they have little body weight to bear and possess the will to move and carry it. It is more difficult for overweight children, but much opportunity for movement helps relieve the problem.

Private conversation

Many of the places where children used to play outdoors have disappeared. Some specially designed housing estates, however, have integral playgrounds, with schools and nurseries amidst child-friendly streets. In some countries, many children still walk to school alone or with friends. As movement in the home is often restricted, play in the open air is vital.

In some countries, it is thought important for children to read and write at an ever younger age, and this actually obstructs young children's need for movement. Yet giving plenty of opportunity for varied physical development lays the foundation for academic work later. In

Priority here for pedestrians and cyclists

Grown-up work

Negotiating a route

physical activity, children gain control of the body and expand large and small motor skills. Lifting, bending, carting heavy objects, stretching and ball play support muscle growth and spatial orientation. Combined with good posture and well-developed small movement skills, this enables the complex right/left coordination necessary for reading and writing, arising more naturally after about 7 years. Climbing, balancing, crawling and hanging upside down also foster spatial awareness and better recognition of, for example, the letters p, b, and numbers 6 and 9. Negotiating slippery surfaces like mud, ice or wet stone slabs challenges balance. Jumping and running help leg muscles and cross-coordination, as does walking which helps children to breathe freely. Small motor skills are extended through using unformed, open-ended playthings with differentiated surfaces like pine cones, and in activities such as cutting, tying, grating, chopping, picking berries and sowing seeds. Bouncing, catching and throwing balls supports physical and cognitive skills.

Bark chips, pebbles, wooden surfaces, gravel and uneven steps offer opportunities for varied movement. Obstacle courses and overgrown paths are exciting. Children love leaping between stepping stones and walking between the lines of paving. Leaping for joy is part of childhood. Children need to make a noise, and movement inevitably often involves shrieks, shouts or gasps, diluted out of doors. Having bare feet (in safe places) is advan-

Youthful agility and experimentation

Muscle use for play-boat building   *Exhilaration*

tageous. The whole body is engaged in swimming, somersaults, cartwheels, swinging, or rolling hoops and wheels. Courage and competence are called on by pushing or pulling heavy objects, slithering up a wind-blown tree, or standing on your head.

One can observe children struggling with spatial concepts. Our rectangular kindergarten painting boards belonged sideways in slatted shelves. At first most 4-year-olds held the board as they had been painting, at the longest sides, while attempting to put it into the narrower slats. Another example: children under 6 or so making biscuits usually cut them irrationally in the middle of the pastry because their whole orientation is towards a central point. In a ring game, children under 5 wander into the centre, and when drawing, they often begin in the middle. Most very young children enjoy dropping things onto the floor, throwing toys out of the pram or off the high chair. They are actually practising spatial awareness, finding a relationship between themselves and their environment. It naturally becomes a game when people start giving them back!

It is good for babies to spend plenty of time flat on the floor or pram on backs but also tummies. This helps spinal development through lifting head and back, stretching and kicking the legs and pushing up on the arms, prerequisites for crawling, standing and walking. In order not to put undue stress on the baby's tender, developing spine, it is valuable to use a sling in which the baby lies nearly flat, mimicking lying on the parent's arm. The back is only strong enough to be upright when the child can sit up straight without support, around 6 months. Of course one also holds the baby upright, supporting the head in the first 3 months or so: yet here one's hands support the back in a responsive way.

Grandpa was looking very keen and excited. He gave his 3-year-old grandson's ball a gentle kick every now and then when it came near. The child was speeding around, kicking it intermittently: round the tree, over the path, back onto the grass, over to Grandpa. When Grandpa switched his baseball cap back to front, the child copied with delight. The child's running, rolling about and jumping up continued with the odd kick, while Grandpa continued with his sporadic 'eager' input, eventually sitting on a bench to 'recover' from all this effort and exertion, but the child ran to the swings and slide, continuing to expend endless bodily energy. His legs didn't even come up to Grandpa's knee, but they were not still at any time during the whole 25 minutes.

There is endless equipment to buy for children's fun. Some may be rather undesirable, such as wheels in the heels of trainers. An experienced osteopath who treats many children told me, 'In my opinion they should be banned. They are disastrous for the joints as the child bangs along on the toes when walking in them, jolting the bones with each step. Riding along on the heels is unnatural and unhelpful.' Roller blades and skates are different as they encourage balance and poise. Battered vehicles and electric scooters don't have anything like the same benefit.

Warming activity in movement

From here onwards, I note snippets from my kindergarten teaching diary's 'plans and reviews'. These are examples of what one can do in class (or at home). I've included the dates of activities to encourage the reader to have a go even when the weather seems inclement. The children were between three-and-a-half and nearly seven. Dates are from various years. Every day in our outdoor times we met aspects of all government 'learning goals' (see Appendix 1).

27 May: Plan: Move wood chips in wheelbarrows up hill to new path. Collect molehill earth to fill in outsides of log-edging on the path, so no one trips over it.

Review: Our local 'builders' in this project, aged between 4 and 7, were enthusiastic, rosy-cheeked people working for the 'community'. This particular task took 3 days, and the children were very eager to be involved.

12–16 March: Gardening Week (we arranged the actual activities daily)

Weed beds	Cut overgrown bit	Finish new onion bed
Make handrail for bridge	behind window	All breaks (food) outside
Dig out compost,	Finish sanding planks	Willow weaving
carry to plants	Prune roses	Lay brick path
Border of willow logs	Light bonfire,	Paint and bake outside
by bridge	cook potatoes	

Gardening Week Review: Friday 16th, Open Day
We had to stay indoors until the visitors had gone but the children had been asking if we could go out afterwards. They loved the week out, playing, working, learning...

Movement outdoors in sun, wind, storm, rain and frost

It is more natural to wrap up and go out if the house is not so warm. TV in cosy bedrooms has also removed the urgency to go out. Who actually chooses to go out in the rain and cold? Yet a day spent indoors can make one grumpy and dissatisfied, so it may be wise to have a quick turn or two outside.

> *Pitter, patter, pitter, patter,*
> *Look at all the rain,*
> *Knocking on the window sill*
> *And on the window pane,*
> *Sounding like the pitter patter*
> *Of little fairy feet*
> *Running down the garden path,*
> *Running down the street.*
>
> *Washing everybody's house*
> *And everybody's shop.*
> *Pitter, patter, pitter, patter,*
> *When is it going to stop?*

Anon

23 January: Beautiful weather, so had picnic on the mosaic terrace on stools.

10 February: Dig and clear bed for onions if weather appropriate. *Review:* Changed plan for today as wet and windy, excellent for walk in puddles!

21 September: *Poured* with rain. Watched cascades from blocked gutters. Fun!

Children can enjoy the wind, especially if you do, and have a windmill, windsock or kite. 'The wind is combing my hair,' said Laurie.

25 January: Fantastic day for expedition: sun and frost. Warm enough for break at sunny log place. Went through bramble tunnel. Sliding sticks across frozen puddles. Great fun. (We spent every Tuesday morning on an 'expedition'.)

Occasionally it happened that we didn't go out for long:
29 January: Expedition day. Went out only for break with warm herb tea and porridge with honey, squeezed into cosy place under large bush. Very damp and cold. Played inside instead.

As rain sustains life, it is wonderful for children to see adults who enjoy and appreciate it. People say, 'It's raining, we can't go out,' including in schools when children have 'wet break'. Central heating makes indoors comfortable. Do older readers remember dragging their clothes into bed in the morning to warm them up? Squeezed together in front of the fire, one's front burned and back froze. The table in a warm kitchen was a centre for meals, homework and chatting. My experience is that children don't mind going out in the rain; they often don't even notice the wet. In countries of extreme drought, dancing and celebrations take place when the rains come. Puddles may be a magnet to children of even 10 or 11. Seeing water pouring out of a blocked drain, a child of 5 sloshing about in his boots said, 'It's pouring puddles.' On walks, one can tell children they can jump in puddles on the way home (thus avoiding wet feet at the start of the trip).

Should we even talk about bad weather? Perhaps one could find a better image that will not put children off, such as 'exhilarating or exciting weather' if it is blowing a gale or pouring cats and dogs!

For a treat in kindergarten, we ran in and out without a coat when it was frosty, asking 'Jack Frost' to help decorate our watercolour paintings on wet paper. When we had finished them, we would pull on our boots and lay the paintings quickly on the frosted grass, still on their boards, away from 'King Sun'. Then there was a lot of excited to-ing and fro-ing to peep—stealthily in case we chased 'Jack Frost' away. What a thrill when beautiful crystalline tracings appeared on the first one. Exquisite revelations continued to appear on others, showing dynamic crystallization. These masterpieces keep their patterns when they dry indoors. To prepare for this stunning phenomenon, put wet watercolour paper, soaked for 5 minutes, onto a board. Using watercolours from tubes which have been diluted with a little water, take a big brush to paint sweeps of colour, avoiding details, over the whole page. For more details of such painting see my book *Well, I Wonder.*★

Clothing to encourage movement

Young children cannot recognize their temperature before the age of 8, so it is a very good idea to dress them warmly, and make sure they are tucked in and buttoned up before going out.

★ See Appendix 2, Further Reading (p. 257).

Whether the weather be fine, or whether the weather be not,
Whether the weather be cold, or whether the weather be hot,
We'll weather the weather, whatever the weather,
Whether we like it or not.

Old rhyme

Children need warmth to develop, grow and move harmoniously. Most children feel happy in warm socks, tights or long johns, scarf, gloves and bobble hat on a chilly day, in street or forest. It is important not to have a gap between trouser legs and socks in cold weather, and to keep feet really warm. Shoe shops and menders sell warm liners.

To make your own felted inner soles, place several layers of sheep's wool in alternate directions, larger than the foot, onto a piece of cotton sheeting; sprinkle on washing-up liquid, roll it up and pour very hot water over it. Using rubber gloves, twist back and forth and squeeze until matted—fun for children when it has cooled. Rinse and cut to size when dry.

We all know how miserable it is to be cold and how it hinders movement, and warm feet really help the whole body. Waists are best kept covered and well tucked in anyway, in order to protect developing inner organs, not easy

Kindergarten winter walk

in these days of short top and low hip fashions. Dungarees are excellent for sheltering the tummy. Keeping gloves on protects hands. Sew them to a piece of elastic or tape pulled through the sleeves. Since they barely move, children in slings, prams and pushchairs need extra clothing, especially for head, legs, feet and hands. Wearing a hat avoids loss of vital warmth. It can be difficult to keep it on! But it *is* important and older children may need reminding. Woven wool is hardwearing, insulating and warm for outside garments. It sheds dirt and absorbs moisture, keeping the wearer dry (that is how sheep survive on wet, cold mountains). There are other natural materials for those who prefer not to wear animal products, such as cotton, hemp and bamboo. Unlike conventional cotton cultivation, organic cotton is not grown using high levels of insecticides. Layers of undergarments keep the body warmer than one thick one. Waterproofs save on washing and mending.

'They get a little bit of water on their trousers or skirt and go into a panic,' said a playgroup leader. This probably filters through from parental anxiety. It can be daunting for parents to let children get wet and messy, especially in a small flat. Yet turning the coat inside out as it is taken off and back again over the bath avoids dirty drips. Muddy clothes can be brushed when dry. A bowl of water and brush by the front door is handy for muddy boots to step into,

Well-clad in rain-filled sandpit

with an old towel to stand on. A waterproof bag or rucksack for collecting things, and secret treasures, is nice. All this dressing takes time, yet its importance is immeasurable. Children benefit from struggling to dress on their own, then enjoy a sense of achievement.

Grandma said to her little grandchild in the pushchair as they left the super-market, 'We're going to wrap you up warmly, darling, as we're going out in the cold.'

'I'm so hot,' said Alexander, 6, pulling off his jumper when he was running about with his friends. I liked to make sure children really *were* hot before they took things off (by putting my hand down the back of their neck); and I got them to put their things on again afterwards, for that is when they get cold without noticing.

Within the family or at school, older children are proud to help the younger. Velcro has generally replaced laces; this makes life easier for parents, yet tying laces helps promote small motor skills and endurance. Zips often take the place of dexterity-furthering buttons, but they get full of sand or earth and split at the bottom. It is good for children to develop

Preparing for outside

the habit of changing their shoes and washing their hands when coming indoors. This also saves floors from dirt and dog's mess. If prettily decorated shoes are kept for 'best', the child will not be hindered in play and movement for fear of spoiling them. Children on farms or abandoned areas, or playing in old bangers or ruins in old clothes are generally blissful, grubby young people with healthy, glowing faces.

Sufficient clothing is essential for any expedition: hat, wool or thermal socks, good footwear (rubber boots do not breathe and can rub), and spare garments. Children feel important with temporarily unwanted jackets tied round the waist: 'real hikers'. If parents fetching their children from my class carried their clothes, I asked with a wink whether they were a coat hanger. They usually laughed and gave the children their belongings (an opportunity to develop muscles and will-power). If children are used to it from very small it is not a problem.

> A parent whose child, now 9, had not wanted to get dirty a few years previously wrote to me: 'We had a wonderful afternoon in the park yesterday, sledging with seven children altogether. It's amazing how gleeful they are in the snow—Lily not caring how wet or muddy she gets. She had the job of moving the compost at school recently—up to her knees in black gold!'
>
> One day I returned at home-time to kindergarten with a crowd of happy but very muddy children, and began to apologize to the parents. They stopped me. 'We think it's wonderful!'

> A kind way to help the younger child to dress well is to make a friendly fuss over dressing dolly first—they enjoy being authoritative in their play: 'Now Bluebell, you'll have gloves next, just like "Mummy" or "Daddy" (i.e. the child) 'or your little hands will freeze and we can't have that, can we?'

What are we wearing outside ourselves? It helps the child to see us doing the same! 'Do your coat up,' said Dad to his 4-year-old, walking along the street and not doing his own up. He had already put hers on for her and given her the hat, but she ignored him. In kindergarten, a doll in a basket in the cloakroom 'told' the children what they should wear when they went outside. They found that appealing, and so did not have to ask me what they should put on. I dressed her in the appropriate clothing for the day but did not change it often, partly as it was an opportunity for giving that repetitive security of sameness that makes children feel good. Waterproofs were often the order of the day in our damp region. What a surprise when she took them off!

Children happy to go out in all weathers enjoy playfully acting out the following poem indoors with a twinkle in their eye, and repeating it as they dance and slosh through the sloppy wetness outdoors.

> *Drip, drip, drip,*
> *What a doleful sound.*
> *Water pouring down from heaven,*
> *Mud upon the ground.*

No more ice on pond or river,
No more lovely snow.
Dismal rain and sloppy wetness
Everywhere I go.

Please, please, Mr Weather Man,
Roll away the dark clouds,
Close your watering can.
Bring the golden sunshine
To bring us hope and cheer,
Telling us their message,
'Spring will soon be here!'

Nora Ward

Sun hats covering the tops of the ears and back of the neck protect from sunstroke and skin cancer. Blond-headed children are of course especially susceptible to burning. It is helpful to have shoulders covered in strong sunshine. A special 'pirate' kerchief can replace a hat, knotted at the four corners. Sun lotion at least factor 30 is recommended for children; their skin is much thinner than ours. Clothing protection is particularly essential to the young baby, especially for the bare head, even indoors. On no account should sun fall in babies' eyes, or on the head without a hat.

Strength and rest

Activity in the fresh air builds up the immune system. In our over-clean, antiseptic, sedentary culture, physical activity is on the decrease. Many teachers feel there is not enough time for moving about outdoors, and sport gets too little attention in many schools. Sport as spectator more than participant, lifts, cars and domestic and garden machinery all contribute to lack of exercise.

Many parents are unsure how much they can ask of their children, like the two laboriously pushing their girls of 4 and 2 up a steep slope in their buggies. At the top, the 4-year-old got out to watch a flautist entertaining the tourists, then danced to the music, twirling for five minutes until her parents put her back in the buggy. Then they hung onto both buggies as they made their way back down the slope. It is advantageous for children to walk up and downhill rather than resting in a pushchair, and this child obviously had no problem moving. What about children who are pushed to the nursery or

Digging in a big hole for a drain

Filling a path edge with molehill earth

pre-school, then run around the playground?

During our afternoon sessions for 3- to 7-year-olds, we had a rest. Some fell asleep. Sometimes we took our mattresses and blankets outside to lie under a tree. In some childcare settings, cots and prams are placed outside, perhaps on a covered veranda. Babies enjoy naps in the garden (with a cat net where necessary). Those in flats can sleep next to the window, out of the draught. I put my own children down in their cot indoors only if it was stormy or very cold or hot, but they invariably screamed until I relented and put

One of my family sleeping, cosy and warm in the snow

them outside, even cosily protected in the snow. Did the disruption to their natural rhythm upset them or did they miss the sky?

Contact with the natural world heals both physically and mentally. Hospital patients feel better if they have beautiful surroundings. City railway stations with flowers and country ones with tended banks of wild plants fortify the traveller. Purposeful play and work in the fresh air enables children to move, eat, live and sleep well. Climbing from one branch to another without falling, hopping from one stone to another, letting the ball roll down the sandcastle or holding a hand in the wind: these all strengthen children.

Movements even express personality. We recognize people by their walk. My young sister asked about her soon-to-be piano teacher, 'Was that the lady who danced along the edge of the sea and got her skirts all wet?' This joyful memory displayed the lady's character so perfectly.

In summary

What a multitude of opportunities there are to help children's movement-related skills out of doors! Work in my garden gives me space to think, feel good in my cheeks and body and enjoy the fruits of my labours. Yet fear is increasingly preventing adults from letting the young enjoy enough work and play outdoors. We will explore this issue further in the next chapter.

3
Risks, Courage, Fear and Freedom from Anxiety

Independence and courage-building

Various health and safety restrictions prevent children from meeting the natural challenges of childhood. Children enjoy 'safely dangerous' adventures and challenges, not cotton wool and kill-joys. They build up sound self-assessment if allowed the freedom to develop physical and life skills, and do not normally go beyond what they can manage. Accidents happen—that is life—but many children are not deterred. Those who can explore their surroundings independently are unlikely to be cowed by any environment, but instead approach each one with courage and inspiration. As their individual spirit flowers, they can rely on themselves, rather than others.

> A mother wrote to me five years after her child left kindergarten:
>
> 'For the benefit of our children, we also need what we would like to avoid: perspectives and approaches that challenge us. I remember worrying a lot about your taking the children out each Tuesday to walk for hours through the woods and across streams in the rain and hot sun. I thought it might be too taxing and had some other nameless fears. Why not a short walk when the weather is fine? But a few months ago Ellen told me how much she had loved it—going out such a long, long way, sometimes having a minute where she felt all alone and adventurous in the beautiful woods, the challenge of crossing streams and walking muddy paths. I think she treasures the memory of those walks and that they helped her become the independent and unafraid person that she is.'

The long, high swings in a woodland adventure park were hung in the trees for a slow, wonderful ride. Wide enough for two people, they were such a joy. After some years of happiness, Health and Safety reared its head: only one at a time; no child under 10; and a full-time warden to ensure no one broke the rules. This resulted in the following exchange, for example: Dad: 'Yes, he's 10.' Son: 'No I'm not, I'm 8.'

> *I see the moon and the moon sees me,*
> *I see the moon and the moon sees me,*
> *I see the moon and the moon sees me,*
> *God loves the moon and God loves me.*

Old rhyme

My four children and I sang this if the moon was shining on the long walk home from shopping on an early winter's evening: heartening, happy. We talked to the cats and said hello to the lamp-posts. Sometimes passers-by wondered at us being out in the dark and cold, but the children stared in wide-eyed, uncomprehending astonishment. Singing or listening to a story under the stars round the campfire is so romantic. The close of day amongst birdsong and other noises of the night brings deep impressions. Light pollution spoils beautiful, deep darkness, but usually at least the moon can be seen. Hearing a story outdoors after dark, snuggled up on a bench, perhaps under an umbrella in the rain is cosy and courage-building. 'It's not so dark when it's a little bit light,' said 4-year-old Theodor, appreciating a lantern's tiny shine.

I was advising in a nursery of 3- and 4-year-olds with a den down a steep slope. The descent began by scrambling over an old iron fence leaning outwards. The children abseiled down several metres hanging onto a thick rope tied to the fence, in the arms of their teacher. She scrambled up again for each one. It was a marvellous, remarkable procedure. The way back was up steep, rickety steps to the said fence which now had to be climbed against its incline. I had known this new teacher as a rather quiet, retiring person, yet now I saw her flourishing and matching protection with the opportunity for courage—what a friend of mine calls 'the shield and the sword'.

Real and unreal threats to safety and development

Many teachers and early years' practitioners feel it is easier and safer to have children indoors. But training teachers to build their confidence and skills, so as to support children's activity outside, will give the children an incomparable gift.

NOTE: ' Practitioner' means a teacher or other adult who works in a childcare or educational setting.

> A student spoke of her pre-school placement, where the children played freely outside every day. She felt they were able to deal with stressful situations and could assess and manage risk. She observed their social skills in negotiating and handling conflicts, and their self-esteem and confidence.

'Danger deep water'

Adults will not let children near water without making some 'risk assessment' first, knowing a small child can drown in 5 centimetres. A sight-impaired person who could not read it would not be there without a guide. Such notices absolve the water-owner of responsibility, but why should they be liable? Have we forgotten how to look after ourselves? Are we losing the capacity for clear judgement and discernment? A risk assessment was made on the gravestones of a church. As some were leaning, they had to be heaved out and laid flat, despite having been there safely for hundreds of years.

> A neighbour said he thought Health and Safety was the death of common sense. Such sentiments are common amongst older people, who remember roaming with friends in parks and woods for hours on end. Stephanie and her sister used to spend whole days cray-fishing off the top of a cliff. An old friend described how she learned to ride a bike at the age of 8. When she got her new bicycle, her dad said, 'Now you can ride your bike along the canal bank.'

Sanie described her 5-year-old falling 6 feet from a tree. She was concerned but he ignored her and went straight back up. It is so difficult to know how anxious we should be. There is every stage between bruising or scratches and broken limbs or even death. One has to judge how likely an accident might be in making risk assessments. How can accidents be avoided if the consequences could be severe? Practitioners take care of children to the best of their ability. I was actually happier taking children out before we had such stringent rules. I was just as careful and aware then, but new laws gave me fears previously absent. 'Health and Safety, Risk Assessments, Children to Adult Ratios, Insurance, Permission' make teachers take a wary step back, however good the intention of such regu-

Self-initiated adventure in the nettles

Skills, risks and courage
(5-year-old, adult nearby)

lations and restrictions. Leaders of groups of children are not normally foolhardy and are glad of parents' trust. It is rather the other way round now; many teachers are stifled by fear, so feel unable to give children vital outdoor experiences. Children need uninterrupted time to engage fully in tree-climbing, den-building or ditch-damming. Space to develop ideas and solve problems is essential.

Sticks are an archetypal children's toy all over the world, lying on the ground just waiting to be picked up. So I taught children how to use them safely. They soon learned that if they didn't hold and use them properly they would be removed. Children naturally argue and

Timid child becoming courageous

squabble; this is early negotiation and social intercourse. In my experience, children fight less out of doors. Boys need a rough and tumble, but aggressive fighting diminishes under the sky. If really necessary, we can step in to shield children from harm or rescue them, for instance if they are really stuck up a tree, a little one can't get off the swing, or they are running into the road. Sherry was afraid to let her class climb trees on their wonderful, long, muddy walks. I encouraged her: 'Do a serious risk assessment, then let the children wipe the slippery mud off their boots on the long grass and allow them to climb to a given height.'

Is it possible that some young people are not sensible because they have not had the chance to practise risks? If they have no chance to enjoy spine-tingling 'safely-risky' adventurous pursuits when younger, they may either become reckless, experimenting with really risky dangers in heights, fire and water, or grow into timid adults. They learn better from first-hand experience what is safe and what is not, rather than from a lecture. I believe that children have spiritual guardians besides their earthly protection from adults. It may even be that adults' excessive fear communicates itself non-verbally to children and makes them *more* likely to come to harm. Of course we should take necessary precautions, but can then leave children's imaginations free to soar as they learn about balance and hone their movement and social skills.

Dangers and obstacles to living learning

Enabling children to be strong and healthy, to size up situations and practise judgement and decision-making is the best way to avoid accidents. Children need security but also the chance to develop a sense of adventure and challenge.

A nurse told me, 'I think most safety rules barmy. How can children learn to take care? It's all this crazy litigation. My children had all sorts of bits of old cars to play with. Children need to play, so we gave up our small garden when they were young. They learnt how to walk through the woods to catch the bus to school every day. But now children are taken to the village school down the road by car. We have to get people off their backsides.' She described how her engineer husband found a plastic water tank, cut doors and windows out, and the children played and played there. No need for expensive, ready-made toys that can only be one thing alone, and so don't allow the imagination free rein.

Naturally mishaps occur, but many children cannot test themselves enough: either they are not allowed because the tool or activity is 'dangerous' or they have little opportunity. Most boys and many girls really want to experiment and do dangerous things. Letting them play with 'junk' can satisfy this need. I would advocate a 'Treasure Island' of old pots and pans, wheels and such like (see chapter 5, p. 85). Of course in a place of education the health and safety officer has to vet it. I believe children are less likely to hurt each other where they can play and work together outdoors.

An infant aged 21 months ran her fingers investigatively along a crack in the shop counter, with no idea it might be unhygienic. Young children have no sense of danger, so they collect (to us) disgusting or unpleasant objects, and are surprised when an adult says, 'Ugh, put that down!' How much can we let go, knowing that in time the child will gain perspectives about what is 'nice' or 'disgusting'? If it is poisonous or otherwise dangerous, naturally we take it away, but always with respect for the child. 'Let's wrap that and put it in my bag to keep it safe.' There may be a complaint but it will be short-lived if the child feels the adult's firm consistency. If an adult reacts strongly, there is a danger that it becomes even more interesting. It can be difficult for parents to know just what *is* unsafe and what they should allow their children. *'Keep off'*—*'Slippery steps'*—*'Dangerous slope'*. We can respond to the child's curiosity by saying: 'Let's hold hands and look at the water/go down together.'

I watched a boy of 2 running about in a public garden. He fell over, then began to get up. But mother, father, grandmother and grandfather all ran to rescue him. Mother said, 'I *told* him not to run. I keep telling him not to run.' When the boy heard her, he began to cry. Grandpa picked him up, but he struggled down and began to run again. Once more: 'You mustn't run! Stop running!' What are little legs for other than running about?

Quiet enjoyment

The rules in some flats did not allow playthings in the communal garden. So the residents got together and agreed a climbing frame would be ideal, which they then bought and set up excitedly and properly according to the instructions. However, the council banned it unless they had an inspector and £2 million public liability insurance. That proved too expensive so they had to remove it.

Concrete and tarmac are hard and unrelenting, and preclude inventiveness. Many accidents, including head injuries, happen in uninspiring school playgrounds. The outdoors is inherently calming, but if unattractive, if it doesn't invite creativity, children may argue and even fight viciously, or display intimidating behaviour. Children can become frustrated and over-boisterous if they do not have inviting play areas. Toys on wheels encourage speed, which increases risks and accidents.

Once we lived in a place where adders were plentiful. A family staying with us went out every morning on a snake hunt, returning quite disappointed if they found none. Once my children were fascinated to see one shedding its skin. They had to wear boots from spring to autumn if not on short grass, and really learned the point when one had his boot bitten. Probably he had stood on the poor creature by mistake, maybe when it was surprised and trying to escape. They are shy, and like many other animals, watch you from their hiding place and try to avoid confrontation. The dangers in nature vary from country to country and children can be taught the necessary rules wherever they live. Water, cliffs, high winds and mountains are obvious, potentially dangerous examples. I believe the natural world is not usually dangerous if treated with thoughtful common sense and respect. Where children are concerned, the most likely dangers in immediate surroundings may lie in the household: from playing with knives or consuming powerful cleaning agents, wrong medicines or glue. Chemicals constitute a hazard in many gardens and farms. People with a dog should pick up excrement. Children are renowned for picking bits up, and even eating it, so this is also a health issue.

An 18-month-old sat on her mother's outstretched legs and filled a bucket with little stones, then tipped them out. Some fell lightly on her mother's legs, who said crossly, 'Don't do that, you hurt me.' Three other children of 18–21 months were very busy throwing stones. 'Carefully, careful with the stones!' called their mothers. But the children did not understand and were annoyed with their mothers for trying to stop their fun. They carried on, unable to throw very hard or far of course. They picked up tiny handfuls of pebbles to throw in the water but they went everywhere. The children flopped onto the shingle, rolled about, fell backwards out of sheer joy and stood up easily, giggling and squeaking. They rolled onto their faces, grabbing stones, not still for a moment. One mother was quite fierce, grabbing her child. 'Stop it, I tell you!' He pulled away from her, kicked her, threw stones at her then ignored her. What was so dangerous about a few little stones thrown so weakly? When he was old enough to throw them better, he would also be old enough to understand and aim them properly.

It is good for children if parents keep a sense of proportion and do not react too strongly in this sort of situation. Anger is also imitated by the child, and may therefore call forth an aggressive response.

Stress outdoors

Stress occurs when children feel overwhelmed, lost or thrown out of their routine. Babies and children may feel frustrated, frightened and even abandoned when they cannot see or hear—and therefore communicate with—the adults pushing them in buggies.

Small babies are happier if kept at home for the first few weeks, not moved

around unless absolutely essential. They find the change upsetting when they
are so new in the world. Their extremely delicate senses are enough reason
not to take them out in the beginning. In and out of the garden is enough, in
my opinion. There is usually a kind neighbour or relation who will do the
shopping or fetch the children from school. Naturally the arrival of a child is a
marvellous thing and proud parents wish to show their baby around.
However, their wisdom in waiting may well be rewarded by a calmer child. I
met a young mother in a huge, noisy store waiting for her husband, holding
her 5-pound, 5-day-old baby on her knee. I admired her child and asked
whether she felt strong enough to be out now, which she answered in the
affirmative, saying he was so small that he was easy to carry about. I naturally
did not want to upset her so kept my thoughts to myself.

Some babies and younger children are distressed when away from home or
travelling, particularly by plane or car, as well as after arrival. The following
observation is not unusual. A 6-month-old cried most of the afternoon on a
Mediterranean beach. For the parents it was no fun either as one or the other
tried to console their over-tired baby, thrown out of his normal surroundings. Naturally there are times when families need to travel, but one can
reduce the upset by keeping familiar things going. Talking about holidays,
Nancy felt young children just want simple situations. They went to the
British coast with their 5- and 7-year-olds. 'Our holiday was absolutely
wonderful, all day long on the beach.'

> Weeping in desperation, a baby about 5 months old was crumpled sideways
> against the side of his forward-facing pushchair. He faced many strangers and the
> din and fumes of heavy traffic. His little legs were flailing about and rubbing
> against each other as if in pain. His father, pushing from behind, was apparently
> oblivious to his child's distress.

A young, pregnant mother looked for a folding pram that would keep her
baby well off the ground and enable him to lie flat and see her, the sky and
trees. She thought the forward-facing pushchair would expose children to
fumes and dirt, especially if low down, and overwhelm them with strangers,
lorries and fast cars coming at them noisily. This might either make them
more aggressive or—the opposite of aggression—withdrawn. A young man
asked me, 'Don't children need stimulation?' Yes, certainly, but how much,
when, of what kind, and at what point does stimulation become overwhelming? And are they not ready to walk when ready for more stimulation?

It has been suggested that many children start school without basic language skills because they have no opportunity to talk when facing away from their 'pusher'. Also, children spend longer in pushchairs and car seats than they used to, along with hours in front of an unresponsive screen. A 2-year-old in the train was grizzling, struggling to get out of the pushchair. 'Stop crying!' The child cried louder and received a slap, so screamed louder. '*Will* you stop crying!' I felt sorry for both: the child who wanted to get out and move, and the mother who didn't know what to do.

> A friend accompanied me on the train. I asked whether he liked to sit facing or with his back to the engine. He said he preferred to travel backwards. 'It's slower.'

Adventure and courage

Many years ago, I worked in a Swiss international mountain school with children of all ages, cultures and backgrounds. For some it was alarming to go on their first three-day hike in the autumn term, or the six-day one in June, sleeping in youth hostels, huts and even hay. But they got to love it! New friendships blossomed, challenges arose and hurdles were overcome.

> 'Hey, did you see that skid?' said William, 9. 'Look at mine,' said George, 7. Both children dropped their bikes and ran to an oak tree. William climbed it quite easily, whereas smaller George needed several attempts to pull himself onto the lowest branch. By now, William was nearly at the top, about 10 metres above ground. He leant back on a branch: 'Arm rest. Foot rest. Lean back. What more could you wish for?' Meanwhile mother had arrived on foot and chatted with her children, just like the days when climbing trees was something no one worried about. William said, 'The tree at Brindle's Corner is not so much fun to climb because they all throw sticks at you.' Did he mean other children or possibly teenagers? Would they do that because they were afraid to climb themselves or had been told not to? I could not imagine that anyone used to climbing would take pleasure in throwing sticks at a fellow climber. When they were down again, William said to George, 'If you want to know my route next time, I'll show you another branch.'
>
> ... A challenge, tree and body geography, left/right consciousness, achievement, a trusting mum: these lads were on top of the world, kings of the sky...

Adventurous trips are beneficial whether in the family, with friends or a group. Priorities change and inspirations awaken. In my kindergarten a child of 4 with developmental delay was afraid of walking through long grass, over logs or in the rain. After a year of daily activities outdoors, he grew to love such adventures. Watching other children scrambling around in all sorts of places fed his imitative nature and encouraged him to try the same. Challenges and chances to experiment are just as important for children with special educational needs as those without. Once, on a kindergarten class hike with children and parents, a big thunderstorm began: everyone made for the protective roof of a wood store. It was heart-warming for the children to see the smiling adults chatting happily, the best possible example of courage in adversity.

Where are all the children?

There is so much fun to be had under the sky, yet many children are cooped up indoors, partly perhaps because their parents are fearful.

We sometimes cycle through a large housing estate at the weekend. Usually not a child is to be seen or heard. One warm Sunday we rode along a quiet residential street where the gardens were visible and cars were parked all along the road, indicating that some families were at home; but only one boy was around. Someone told me her sons, now young adults, had played outdoors a lot, off on their bikes and messing around with friends. 'Children don't do it now. They are indoors watching videos and playing computer games. The roads are clogged up as people fill their garages with junk, and many people have two cars so the roadsides are full up and some are parked half on the pavement.' Naturally younger children need to be within sight or hearing of an adult so they can play safely. Older children can play four-square and other games sensibly on

5 pm, no child to be seen

quiet roads if they have nowhere else to go. Singing games, which are all but vanished now, were typically played on the neighbourhood road. They are enjoying a small revival in some schools. Of course, generally roads are not for play, but the increase in traffic is one reason why children are being driven indoors. It can be difficult to travel around safely on a bicycle because of the traffic. Many people have become worried about child molestation. Yet statistics show that there are probably no more cases now than there used to be, but these are just more widely publicized. Eighty per cent of child abuse happens at home. If parents do not want to let their children out but have a garden, however small, they can make the best use of it. A garden can be a haven for children, and there are suggestions relating to this later in the book.

Protection and control, reassurance and safety

Many children live in an increasingly restrictive environment. If they make a noise, they may be shouted at and told to go away. The pre-school setting or school may be the only place where they are outdoors. They need places to go, skateboard parks, benches to sit and chat, areas for ball and other games, adventure playgrounds, open spaces. We can take courage and keep our common sense intact without ignoring what is safe and healthy. Where is the healthy balance between being over-protective and unconcerned? I am convinced that our enthusiasm, awareness, common sense and love help protect the children in our care.

With an easterly gale, it could be bitterly cold in winter by the sea where we lived, but my children and I, well wrapped up, always enjoyed going there after shopping. Some children are lucky enough to have trusting parents who let them sleep in a tent or tree house. Some friends' children dug themselves a den at the bottom of the garden and furnished it; they spent whole days and nights there. Many children used to be sent off to play with a picnic, sometimes staying out all day and getting up to awe-inspiring adventures. Mobile phones can be a comfort to parents but they cannot replace trust. It is rare for anything untoward to happen, especially if children are with others. Janie waited until her child was 10 before she let her cross the fast, traffic-filled road alone, because she believed children have to reach a certain age before judging such speed and distance. Parents will judge indi-vidually at what age their child is capable of assessing the dangers of their local roads. Soft netting is a thoughtful replacement for 'No Ball Games'.

Naturally one has to keep one's own children or those of others under control for their own safety. Teachers and leaders find their own ways of holding the reins and establishing clear rules from the beginning. When becoming more aware and safe, children over 6 respond to an authoritative approach in family or class. I found a playful way more effective with younger children, and speech rhythms they could imitate. For example, chanting while going along the pavement, with appropriate actions: 'One, two, go, hop, Watch your toe, hop, Put it down, hop, We're in town, hop.' Towards the crossing: 'Some-thing's com-ing, Hop, hop, hop. All stand still now, Stop, stop, stop.' You can make the noises of the traffic going by before you cross, raising awareness: bus: 'Brrrrrrrrrm'; sports car: 'Wheeeeeeow'; van: 'Grr- Grr- Grr-'; bicycle: 'Phoo, Phoo, Phoo', and so on, then cross safely. Amongst other strategies, I found if, for instance, a child started to run off, 'Are you going to do that again?' in a serious voice was constructive: not threatening but challenging and firm. If you are in a large open space, in which young children may feel like running off, you can run here and there and twirl round and about. Since, up to at least 7, they are still imitative, they are likely to copy you and stay near to join in the fun. If some go off the wrong way on purpose, you can turn round and go another way to surprise them. This is very effective and they normally come back. At about 6, children like to push ahead or hang back. They like the following game (which the whole group can join in): 'You can run as far as … (hesitating) that pile of leaves/the post/the big tree/the mossy bank. That gives them a challenge and sets a boundary. I also had a signal: if children ran ahead I would call 'Uh-Oh' and they'd come back. It saved a lot of words and annoyance. The other children sometimes called 'Uh-Oh' too if someone went off. When a group is new and not yet settled, children need other children as partners until they and the adults feel rules and good habits are set. On the road and where there is traffic, of course children must walk in an orderly fashion. Road sense develops better by walking than in a car.

'Pony-reins' can be taken out on walks so children can play horses. One can say to a new, young child in a group who is prone to running away, 'You may be my pony today.' They are usually glad to be and it makes them safe without bothering anyone else. Of course this must not be used to restrain a child, but just as a game. Grabbing children, shouting angrily or making them afraid is not the way to stop them running off. This tends to happen if there are too few limits and boundaries at home or they are unused to walking.

Some practitioners do not take children on walks for fear of children running away, but this is a pity for the rest.

> To form a simple play-rein, sew a 5-cm-wide loop, 2 metres long, from strips of cloth. It can also be of crocheted, plaited or twisted cord, decorated with small bells. Place it across the back of the neck, the front of the shoulders and back under the armpits.

Parents need to know the policy for children leaving the premises, and sign a form to give permission. They like to know about the provisions made, staffing, what children need to take with them, and perhaps more about the setting or school and its philosophy. Parents not used to taking their children out feel better if they know what happens and the reasons for doing it. Realizing how healthy it is for children to go beyond the school gate makes it easier for parents to support staff with children in their care. Uncertain parents may like to ask questions to calm themselves, and staff will normally be happy to answer them. Some parent education by the school may be necessary.

Each setting or school makes risk assessments and decides on adult to pupil ratios. Someone with a current paediatric first aid certificate accompanies excursions. Practitioners ensure someone knows where they are going. With car trips, there need to be comprehensive insurance policies and clean driving licences. All adults going out with the children will agree amongst themselves beforehand who takes on which responsibility. Each adult might have a rucksack and between them there will be a list of children present, a mobile phone with relevant school and parent numbers and first aid pack. Other items will include water, toilet paper, clean rags, a trowel, penknife, string, spare pants and socks. One can take cleansing wipes but, because of their negative environmental impact, I prefer soap and clean water. For a fire, you need extra water and burns remedies for accidents which will hopefully never happen. One adult goes ahead, one behind, a third between. Some classes walk in pairs, others in single file, younger ones possibly holding onto a rope. Well-disciplined children may walk more freely, even young ones. It is wise to count children under 7 or 8 frequently. Older children are naturally more independent and capable, so need less close supervision.

When trips are regular, it will become natural to keep to the same arrangements. That sameness is a comfort for the children, and also reassuring to the adults. Children need to be with confident adults, and are likely to behave well if they feel secure with them. With other adults they trust and a class they know well, teachers will be rewarded with happy excursions. Some adults need a great deal of courage to take children on outings. This may be partly due to media alarmism and safety issues, but it might be because they are generally fearful themselves. A few quiet thoughts the evening and morning before a trip can help overcome one's own fears.

In earlier years, I used to find celebrating festivals with parents something of an ordeal. However, I gradually realized that if I prepared every possible detail—for example by giving the parents song sheets beforehand, arranging what the assistants' responsibilities were, how much space to leave between chairs, where latecomers could sit, where little vases of flowers should stand, what order things would happen in and where buckets of water would be if there were candles and so on—then the festival would take care of itself and something beautiful could happen. The same can apply to taking children out: if every practical detail is taken care of in advance and every adult knows exactly what his or her responsibilities are, then the children will feel good, and a lovely time will be had (even when taking a bunch of children into the woods!). The first trip could be very simple, for example an 'adventure' around the inside of the perimeter fence with a picnic on the way. The next might be the same but with an additional adventure 100 yards outside the fence and back, just slowly 'pushing the boundaries'. Anyone misbehaving can be required to stay next to an adult. They soon learn. I believe that if older children are well prepared and know you trust them to behave sensibly, they will—they like to go out.

Struggles and strengths

Children need to be free from anxiety so they can learn to embrace tricky situations with courage and flexible thinking. Under 6 or so the relationship between adult and child is different; here the trust and willingness is unconscious, and children simply 'imbibe' an adult's certainty and guidance.

Children experience the best image of bravery when struggling to keep lanterns alight in rainy, windy autumn lantern festivals, or singing through the darkness whilst not losing each other. Such adventures really teach children about the world. Children can expand their horizons by being exposed to the unplanned, unknown. I think they want to be challenged by

9 Sticks 'in conversation' lying on red earth

10 Colour for joyful play

11 My family

12 Rhubarb houses

13 Rhubarb crumble

14 Ditch, bridges and play house

15 Regular kindergarten picnic

16 *Tending the bread oven fire*

17 *Secret camp of poles and cloths*

18 *Returning the tiny frogs*

unpredictability and uncertainty. What about being lost in the mist? If people are well kitted out and have a map and compass, listen to the weather forecast and ask the locals, they reduce the risk and trouble of getting lost.

In summary

We can't be sure of anything in life. Losing our way and getting hurt is part of human experience. You often become all the stronger for your struggles. I really believe that exposure when young to difficult physical situations—and getting out of them again—lays the ground for courage and ingenuity in adulthood. If children are busy they can be happy outside all day long, only coming in if they are tired, too cold or hot, have homework, or for meals. As we shall see in the next chapter, allowing time and space for free play gives the developing human being an encyclopedia of inner reserves.

4
CULTIVATING PLAY AND IMAGINATION
OUTDOORS

A Silver Night

The stars are silver,
The moon is bright,
O! What a beautiful, beautiful sight.
The sky is cloudless,
The earth is alight,
This is a universe in all its might.

Clare Mullan, aged 8

Inspirational activity

The child's world of wonder, beauty and discovery flows into creative expressions in outdoor play. Creativity is an affair of the limbs—of physical challenge and discovery—as well as head and heart. Truly free play draws on and strengthens inner resources and self-reliance, and the natural environment offers an endless playground where the imagination can spread its wings.

23 December. Everyone played with leaves, pine cones and needles, holes in the ground, sticks large and small, bits of wood, trees, stones and moss: their 'toys'.

12 November. Wonderful imaginative and sociable work and play round the bushes.

Great art stimulates the imagination. The two figures on Colour Plate 9 could be ancient cave art or a modern canvas. Yet they are just sticks on the ground. They might generate playful activity in children who would walk and dance them about, let them talk and sing, while finding more 'props' for their puppet story. Coming across a 'fairy ring' of mushrooms in the grass, a child said, 'Maybe they sleep on them.' 'It's like the story of the little green button,' said another. How lovely to be under a colourful autumn tree shedding its leaves on a sunny, blue-sky day, throwing them up, watching them fall, rolling and hiding in them. Standing under a fruit tree shedding its spring blossom seems like fairyland, with confetti at an elves' wedding. Treasures abound: bees with tiny pollen sacs; a frog on a water-lily leaf. Children like making collections, perhaps of tree seeds of extraordinary diversity: the minute, winged birch, plump acorns, ash keys or in cedar cones. Leaves, flowers, stones and diverse grasses inspire collages and other art forms. Much painting, drawing, modelling, embroidery, tapestry and composition have been inspired by nature.

'I can run miles-of-hour,' said a 5-year-old, twirling merrily and dancing along the path. Then a girl about 15 months scraped up little stones from the gravel. What did she see? Colours? Shapes? Textures? Sparkles? It was lovely that her parents let her get quite dirty and accepted her 'gifts'.

A 6-year-old was making an Easter puppet show on the grass and noticed she had no eggs. 'Here are some,' said Michael, also 6, picking up some pebbles.

Trees provide playrooms

There is so much in nature to initiate play: pebbles, tree roots, leaves ... Children who are used to occupying themselves without adult guidance often recreate and extend their experiences. One day, my kindergarten assistant secretly made a fairy garden with dry grass, berries and flowers under a hawthorn tree. Filled with surprise and wonder, the children made several themselves afterwards, inviting the fairies to come.

Some playgroup children had grown rhubarb. Then they cut it and marched about, holding it over their heads with squeals and giggles. 'Jimmy says we could make a house

Intriguing place

out of rhubarb!' They washed, chopped and cooked it for a delicious crumble. Was this play or work? *(See Plates 12 & 13)* Children were sifting compost with great gusto and aplomb: 'We've no time to play!' Describing their pond-clearing excitedly and proudly, they said: 'We didn't have time to play.' Two 6-year-olds discussed their digging. 'Are we working or are we playing?'—pause for thought—'We're working *and* we're playing.'

Children benefit from makeshift articles, and enjoy pulling or pushing large cardboard boxes, wheels and pulleys, logs on a rope, old buggies or branches. They make up games, like pushing a cart to one another and throwing beanbags in as it goes by. Two 4-year-olds pulled two large, long logs along in a cart. To the uninitiated they replied: 'They're not *sausages*. They're *babies*.' They found two more logs. 'Now we've got four babies. Two boys and two girls.' Experiential play is fruit for intellectual develop-ment and harmonious social life. Children putting planks, string and cloth together for an imaginary raft to sail on the 'ocean' are using hands and feet, lively thinking, heart's passion, imagination, enthusiasm and creative socia-bility. Arguments are tackled with strong feelings and possibly quite creative language. They make use of their developing inventiveness and ingenuity,

Treasures . . .

Blissful playthings

Exciting sawmill

taking simple risks as they handle heavy wood and organize each other with flexibility and a high degree of involvement. Children who watch adults building, or any other indoor or outdoor activity, are likely to make this the focus of their play. Machinery is often noisy but extremely interesting.

> *25 May*: Examined digger and excavator and dumper truck. The children played diggers for the next few days, revisiting and consolidating their impressions.

Time for unstructured play; hindrances to creativity

Being in nature relieves children of some of the negative aspects school can bring: tarmac and competition, tables and chairs, paper and pencils. It thus frees them from possible memories of unhappy and unsuccessful formal learning. It refreshes them and opens up a new world as they play, teaching them living sciences: biology, astronomy, zoology, geology, botany, physics and chemistry as well as history and geography. Children introduced to a world where there is nothing much except nature gradually catch on: their innate originality dawns on them again.

Many children would be happy all day long under the sky, particularly the practically inclined. Outdoor-loving Theo, 6, said plaintively 'Who invented school?'

A mother chatted outside the school gate. She wished her children would join the many staying for structured after-school care. 'My children don't want to stay. I can't get them to stay, *ever*. They just want to come home and play.' Not everyone is able to be at home after school, but how good it was that these children could be free rather than—yet again—involved in organized activity.

Joanne, 6, sat in front of children's TV. It was 8 o'clock on a beautiful September morning by the sea, the garden and beach under her nose. How many children are missing out on valuable playtime? It is becoming increasingly common for children, even as young as 3, to forget how to play well because unhelpful images are 'playing' in their minds. They may have toys which act and speak and look like what they are meant to be, leaving little space for resourcefulness. You can see creativity and imagination at work in the way a child uses an object as many different things (e.g. a stick can, in turn, become a sword, a wand, a hole-maker, a tree, etc., etc.). I have observed such activity so frequently, for example children using plates and mats as mobile phones, and cushions upright and flat on a chair as a computer.

A friend described how her children used to visit a farm with various animals, then finish up with a tractor-trailer ride up a steep hill. At the top they would all jump out to play in bushes and bracken. Yet when she visited recently she saw a group of children arrive who remained sitting in the trailer. After some encouragement they climbed out, but still did not know what to do. Apparently this is now common on the farm.

When deeply absorbed in play, children may be quite unaware of what else is going on. 'Get up and stand still!' shouted a frustrated playground assistant to some boys of 10 and 11 building with newly supplied logs and boards, while she tried to get all the children together after break. 'The bell has gone, why don't you listen?' The non-compliant children looked up, bemused. 'I didn't hear the bell,' said one.

Nature offers children beauty and honesty, nourishing their moral nature. Either the potential or conversely the inability to imagine has a profound influence on adult thought and activity. Over-stimulated chil-

Hats are made for play

dren may find it difficult to listen or concentrate. Yet if left to their own devices, they may begin to play freely and even use objects without any particular shape or form. Out of doors there is a marvellous opportunity to do just this, for in the unspoilt child's mind everything can become anything. Battery-operated toys deprive children of movement and imagination, since such toys do the moving and representation themselves.

A boy about 8 found a paddle by the river and walked along, shouldering both his ten foot long stick and the paddle. He put both down and pushed the stick around with the paddle. Then he threw the paddle into the water and continued on his journey just with the stick, obviously the more valuable possession.

Tree roots, nature's playthings (Sheffield Park Garden, National Trust)

Mud is for girls and boys

Mostly, but not only, boys enjoy a mud-ball play-fight. 'Come back! Come out of there, come here will you, out of that mud!' Those 10- and 12-year-old brothers were enjoying banging each other's two-foot sticks and drawing pictures in the mud with them.

Angela, 12, with a beautiful heath on her doorstep, said, 'I'm bored,' and rarely went out to play. She had hours of homework, so there was little time or strength left for resourcefulness. Young people who have not had the opportunity to be freely creative in childhood, and who are bored and either not stretched enough or cannot cope at school, school 'failures', may gather round pubs and clubs and hang about on the streets, seeking escape in alcohol and drugs, their thwarted powers of invention transformed into hooliganism. This can be the case even in rural villages. Some places have excellent skateboard and bike parks and youth clubs, but it can be difficult to raise enough money for them. Funding and lack of training is often a problem for many voluntary youth organizations. Recognizing troubles faced by the young, the UK government has a strategy for young people called 'Youth Matters'. Local Authorities with expertise in working with teenagers are developing successful partnerships termed 'Youth Offers' with knowledgeable groups such as the Wildlife Trusts. Other countries have their own, similar schemes.

A girl of 7 with a big toothless grin ran down a steep slope to a swing at an outdoor restaurant, swung a few times, ran into the playhouse nearby, collected a teapot and jug, ran up the hill to the restaurant to fill them with water, ran downhill again holding them out sideways (forgetting in her eagerness to hold them properly, so the jug emptied quickly and the teapot poured out all the way), left them in the playhouse and ran up the hill again, puffing as she could only manage to walk the last bit—and if you are not left feeling a bit puffed yourself after reading this, then I have not described it well. She was simply engaged in a child's busy, joyful play. The phenomenon of the emptying jug and teapot are typical of the younger child engaged in a process, not bothered about the result.

Philip's play house

When does imaginative play end? Does it ever? A girl of about 10 lingered behind her family. Thinking she was unobserved, she gave a shy, intimate low wave to something amongst tall plants in a stream, then broke out of her reverie to follow her parents. The more we allow space for unstructured play in childhood, the more we can play as adults with ideas and practicalities, reaching solutions and giving social and artistic gifts to the world. As an adult, Philip still retained the playful imagination that allowed him to create a fantastic two-storey castle of recycled bits and pieces for his children, in their pocket-handkerchief London garden.

Entertainment and directed play

Real play is individually inspired. Wasteland and simple toys like upturned brooms for hobby horses used to provide children with endless occupation, yet such traditional free play is now being replaced by organized, guided play, specialized equipment and 'entertainment'. There are superb wildlife programmes on TV, yet adults still need to be sensitive to the developmental age of the children before letting them watch. It takes children several years to become familiar with the geography, flora and fauna in their environment, so there is plenty of time to introduce them to icebergs, cheetahs and tree frogs.

In a typical children's cartoon, humanized flowers, reptiles and insects were making mud pies in the rain under a blue sky. I wondered how many children watching would actually play in the rain (under a blue sky?) and make mud pies themselves. There is a manipulative, addictive quality to electro-visual media. Fun and joyful play outside is *healthily* addictive. Many children prefer to be outside, away from programmed, structured play.

What is child-appropriate entertainment? The mother of twins of 2 and a boy of 4 said, 'We have to get your passports, or we can't go to Disneyland.' 'I haven't got a passport!' said the boy. 'Yes, you have!'—'No, I haven't.'—'Yes, you've got yours already!'—'No, I haven't!' What did the child understand about Disneyland or a passport? Later I was talking to some new neighbours. It was December and there were tiny white Christmas lights on a bush. Mother said, 'We like looking at the little lights. Glen (6) has been telling me about your birch trees.' Such 'small' things can be more lastingly memorable than a long trip involving passports and big sensations. Self-discovered objects and situations are so valuable. 'What's that?' asked a 4-year-old. 'What?' asked Mum. 'That,' said the child, pointing. 'What?'—'It's very high.'—'Oh, you mean the church tower!' Mum hadn't seen anything particular amongst the row of houses and taller buildings.

Education in and after school may deprive children of their natural playtime and curiosity-arousing instincts. 'Purposeful learning' is directed by staff, rather than children being individually purposeful and resourceful. Many parents spend large amounts of money to amuse their children during the long summer holidays, worried about them getting bored. Activity holidays are mushrooming. Even beautiful gardens and parks have assumed teaching roles, offering guided trails, workbooks and activities. This is a good idea, yet are children missing something by following such prescribed tracks? Their attention and concentration may be absorbed in ticking off the next goal rather than truly observing, standing and staring. When are children *really* ready to describe flowers, their scent, texture, size and colour, count the number of petals and leaves, and respond to the challenge of drawings trees or insects? Might they simply learn through self-motivated observation and activity, discovering at first hand, in direct, self-determined involvement, the foundations of botanical and zoological knowledge?

There are many remarkable and innovative centres and *specifically* educational courses for children in schools and clubs, like those run in the UK by the Royal Society for the Protection of Birds (RSPB), Wildlife Trusts, National Trust and County Councils (see Appendix 2). Some of these centres are within or close to cities and provide the children with a breath of fresh air and totally different experience on their doorstep. Teachers often notice a difference and improvement in children after such a visit. Farm walks arouse curiosity and interest for children. I would take young children to visit a farm rather than the zoo: just as fascinating but more familiar.

A pre-school makes regular field trips, including an annual journey to the zoo 100 miles away. I wondered whether those children would be just as happy playing in the local woods. Is it really necessary to drive a long way to see something still 'foreign' to their small world? Children enjoy simple pleasures. A 10-year-old: 'My mum takes me for treats. The park, by 75 bus, is a lovely place to go in spring with avenues of huge horse chestnut trees, avenues of them, all pink and white blossom. Sometimes she takes me on a boat down the river to Greenwich. Then we get out and walk up the hill to the Observatory.' With children over 5 or so, one can enjoy very exciting walks such as in the darkening evening mist to an abandoned slate quarry on a Welsh hillside, finding ruined cottages and sheep bones on the way. There are glorious places to discover not far from home wherever children live all over the world, for example sea cliffs, huge trees in parks or small and large waterfalls. Streams, canals and rivers are always a joy. Even in a dry riverbed there are stones and plants to be explored (take care if it rains heavily in case of flash floods).

When visiting theme parks and other outdoor attractions, one may like to take a picnic, as many have nutritionally poor food on offer. Planning in some free time as well as scheduled activity is also a good idea.

Time and opportunity to play in all seasons

One very rainy day, the children were having a great time in the partially flooded sandpit. I helped digging castles and moats. Franny, 6, gazed up at me and said, 'You're like a big child.' However, our ability to think ahead and organize our mental concepts gets in the way of the free flow that lives in the child's mind. We can be the customer if they want us to play shops, or the sick baby if they want to be a Mummy or Daddy, but the game will mainly be led by the child. When not planned for learning by adults, play changes continually like flowing water and the wind. Just as their bodies are constantly moving, so do their minds, driven by their incredible, innate creativity. In old paintings one often sees angels on the earth, walking amongst human beings. When children are singing and playing happily, it is easy to imagine angels playing amongst them too. There's a special atmosphere surrounding a child intensely involved in imaginative play: a wondrous, hushed absorption.

20 October: Walk, to find 'treasures' to put in big flat basket: leaves, nuts, seeds, berries. Basket full of glorious colours. Will press leaves for window transparencies and lanterns. Children entertained themselves jumping back and forth across ditch many times. Story sitting on benches outside shed.

We enjoyed our playful 'ring-times' under the sky, the 20 or 30 minutes of action songs and verses we did every day. When it rained we put a rainy slant to some of the songs. If it was frosty, our extra, busy activity made us hot.

15 January: Expedition day. The children carried planks for sitting on, all the way to the fire site (a mile). Once there, they went off to play in self-forming small groups. Good social activity within natural environment. Some found roots of a tree to shelter in as gnomes; others went under bushes to make a house or climbed low trees. Some helped with building fire. Several stood staring at it. Harmonious, active morning. Children healthily tired.

21 January: Raked and swept sand, made patterns.

8 February: The sandpit was frozen. Exciting. The children 'skated' on it.

11 February: Fun in sandpit, water several inches deep from overnight rain not yet drained away. Those with boots to the knee, tights and two pairs of socks were allowed in.

26 April: Whole class played under big bush for three quarters of an hour. Very happy.

3 July: Promised the children to play in sandpit first thing tomorrow. *Review following day*: Rained cats and dogs but the children still wanted 'to play on the beach'. They made a moat, bridges, tunnel and a decorated castle.

Nothing much

Play with 'nothing much', i.e. unrepresentative toys, creates resource-fulness in the child, surely ever more essential on our threatened planet. Some of other people's litter on the beach or anywhere else may provide play material for children. Collecting it for the recycling centre does the environment a favour, and shows the child an attitude of respect and care.

One holiday, four children aged 7 to 14 played for some hours every day on the sturdy flat roof of their rented cottage, making houses with bits and pieces of brick, tile and 'rubbish' they found. Left to their own devices, children seize every opportunity to be creative. Seaweed, shells, driftwood, sand and pebbles are often transported home from the beach. Sticks, leaves, a rubber band and lumps of dried mud may accompany the child back from a walk. If children can play like this, why should they need anything more complicated at home? Besides developing inventiveness, they are learning for instance physical and mathematical properties: the qualities of material, weight and height comparisons, categorization. By throwing stones into the sea, the child learns about space orientation, colour, texture and response of material. Throwing stones at an old tin involves judgement and physical skill. Sculpting mud is also a scientific experience; it barely moves when cold and stiff but is sloppy and pliable when warm. For decorating sandcastles and making roads, children collect translucent stones, smoothed glass 'jewels' and rubbish: yoghurt pots, blackened shoes, bits of rope or pieces of broken polystyrene. You can hoist a sail on the beach (or anywhere) to sail into the far distance: push a (driftwood) stick or ferrule of a folded brolly into the ground, with towel attached or an old piece of rag tied on, using (washed up) bits of string for rigging. If you have been building castles with flotsam and jetsam, please take whatever is litter home or to a recycling centre. Take care

Flotsam and jetsam

with tar and containers that may have held toxins, but take them too. If you go to a shingle beach, hunt for a hag-stone (one with a hole) to hang up outside the door; it keeps the witches away, they say (we have certainly been safe so far!).

> 'This *is* a house,' said 4-year-old Oliver indignantly. 'No, it's a *fire engine*,' insisted the 5- and 6-year-olds. 'I got here first, so it's a house,' said Oliver, not to be beaten by his superiors. 'No, *we* got here first, so it's a *fire engine*.' One child touched a bolt on the climbing structure: 'If you press the button it becomes a fire engine. If you press it again, it's a house.' All was peaceful: house and fire engine co-existed contentedly.

A visiting kindergarten student was struck by the way the children filtered out and quickly found something to occupy themselves without instruction. They knew every corner of their garden and were contented and calm, obviously enjoying whatever they were engaged in. She noted they were all interested in her visit, wanting to talk, share and give her a tour of the garden.

If offered unformed objects and opportunities without direction, children create an inspirational, constructive world. So when the rain mixed with the resin of a pine tree and a frothy mixture ran down the trunk, the children reckoned it was Mrs Washing emptying her bowl. 'How is she doing her rinsing?' 'She's holding it out in the rain!' They liked me to open my mouth to the sky to 'drink' the rain. Naturally they did likewise, feeling the tingling on the tongue. 'I've got fizzy orange juice.' 'I've got wobble-bobble juice.'

You can easily make a swing in the woods. Attach a stick to a piece of string, which is tied to the end of a rope strong enough to swing on (taken with you just in case). Throw the stick over a strong branch and catch it the other side, pulling the rope with it. Tie this end of the rope round the tree trunk or some stable object, tie a stout stick to the other end to sit on and hey—presto!—you have a wonderful plaything.

> A girl of 11 leapt over a soggy track with the aid of a stick as long as herself which she had been carrying, saying: 'This is where sticks come in handy.'
>
> 'It's a hundred years old! It *says!*' Two excited 'geologists' of about 6 and 8 had made this historic discovery on scrambling up a sandstone boulder. 'Come up, Mum, Dad! It *is*, the rock is a *hundred* years old, it *says*, right *here!*' (1907 etched there certainly looked ancient after a hundred years of erosion . . .)

Swing made in a moment

Stories outdoors

Stories told outdoors have a special quality. You can make them up, using the simplest elements and incorporating whatever you see around you. This takes some courage to begin with, but a child's rapt attention will keep you going . . .

Lying on your back under the sky, gazing at the clouds sailing by: 'The white horse flew by so fast that his tail caught in the hedge and he had to leave it behind . . .'

'This is our rug,' said some children when they sat on the soft green grass for their story. Children love stories from nature, where for instance trees speak and animals help each other, such as the old Chinese tale of 'The Rabbit and the Carrot'. What better place to tell them than outside, with a breeze in your hair under a tree or on a hillock? If you can remember them, you do not even have to carry a book with you. Or just make up your own. Tell them somewhere the children can sit down and be comfortable. A narrative sustains tired children walking home. There was a place I sometimes used to hike with my kindergarten, about two miles away, to the top of a long hill from where you could see 'the whole wide world'. The children loved to hear the story up there of 'How Six Men Got On in the World' (Grimm Brothers). St Michael's kindergarten in London (see cover) is on the fourth floor with many flights of stairs; the children climb down to their delightful, tiny garden mid-morning. After playtime there, they go happily into a corner covered with a tarpaulin and sit on logs for their story, come rain, shine, snow or blow.

Children do love to listen to a story being read to them and to look at the pictures. Many illustrations are not very artistic, however, and may give the child harsh or even frightening images. If the adult tells the story, children are free to make their own inner pictures. In my experience I would say their listening can be even richer and more intense if a story is told, and the

On top of the world

relationship between adult and child may be even closer. However, the strong images from TV or video stories may get in the way of the child's imagination. In such cases I have found it helpful to show what I would call beautiful illustrations while still *telling* that same story, to help release the child from disturbing inner images. Nancy Mellon (see Appendix 2) has written extensively on storytelling. Wonderful picture books can be found, such as those produced by the publisher Floris Books.

'We would like to read stories to our children, but we don't have any books.' This family had plenty of videos, computer games and time spent indoors. Reading to them would of course be wonderful. Telling stories would enliven their imaginations, especially outdoors. Another couple wanted to get rid of the TV, so they told their children it was broken. They took it to the church bazaar but the children saw it for sale there. 'But it's broken,' they reminded their parents...

Story time

Horse's tail

The 'top of the world'

Puppet plays

It is lovely to create a puppet show outdoors, especially if it is a surprise. Your hat or some pine cones moved gently about in your hands do equally well if you have no 'proper' puppets to hand. Children with lively imaginations fill in the details. If you have never done this, have a go! Children unused to it will soon be fascinated, I am sure.

> Lulu, nearly 6, laid down a silky green cloth folded into a rectangle. 'This is the desert where all lovely green grass grows and all flowers and things.' She put a pink folded silky rectangle on top, then a blue. 'This is very special blue grass.' She laid a red rectangle down over a wooden log. 'This is a special red castle.' Then she carefully picked up her puppets and her story unfolded...

Judy made a puppet play of Snow White and the Seven Dwarves, with piles of pine needles for the seven hills amongst tiny paths she'd scraped clean. The pine cone dwarves, twig queen and white feather representing Snow White fitted in her pocket to take home afterwards. If you draw out some thin coloured cloths very slowly from your pocket or rucksack, children are filled with awed anticipation. Spread them around you quietly as 'scenery', offering them to the children next to you to put on their laps also. Producing

Creating a puppet show

Outdoor puppet show

simple puppets out of your other pocket, just begin. Puppet plays of the children's invention are likely to follow soon. It is enchanting to present a little show for a festival outdoors, made more special by preparing the space with the children beforehand, by tidying and decorating. Make sure there is room for children and elderly folk to sit. Parents will not mind standing for ten minutes. It is fitting to start with some simple instrumental music and to sing, which creates a magical mood in the dark at a lantern festival, lit only by little lamps and sometimes a moon.

Drama

Children enjoy acting in the open air. For younger children, plays or circle times can happen outside wherever you are, always maintaining the same rhythmical daily pattern.

Simple rhymes with corresponding actions engage little ones, whereas older children may want to prepare scenery for a play. Sometimes you can use the landscape to advantage (for instance, wandering amongst small trees or bushes for a fairy-tale forest). We practised our play one day on undulating ground. Up the hill we went to begin the tale, then down as the story unfolded about the adventures a boy had while running downhill. 'The story's coming true!' said several. While we wound around molehills when singing our play of Snow White, they said: 'The seven hills!' When doing our nativity play outside, we saw my male assistant tending the bread oven, which was under a little roof. 'There's Joseph!' they said.

Music-making outside

Music comes from the heart; what could be more lovely than a parent singing to a child under the sky.

> *Tom he was a piper's son,*
> *He used to play when he was young.*
> *But all the tunes that he could play*
> *Were over the hills and far away.*
> *Over the hills and a long way off,*
> *The wind shall blow my top-knot off.*

Old rhyme

A song can also make the way home shorter. The young child will want it repeated many times until the parents are sick of it but the child wants it *again*. Older children will sing different songs or a round, perhaps something from school or the latest from the charts. Singing games outdoors are especially fun. Children love the following, ever-repeating old rhyme, especially on a windy walk. It helps them feel secure.

> *There was an old man called Michael Finigin,*
> *He grew whiskers on his chinigin.*
> *The wind came out and blew them inigin,*
> *Poor old Michael Finigin, Beginigin,*

(Repeat from the beginning)

Old rhyme

It is easy to form an imaginary orchestra outside with children. Pick up a twig or cone and tootle on it, and soon all sorts of interesting instruments will play around you. It is fun to make a blade of grass squeak, an owl hoot in cupped hands or whistle between the fingers. Children like to make different sounds and rhythms by banging things together or on an upturned bucket or arranging bits of wood and stones on the ground to make a xylophone.

When I was expecting my fourth child, we got lost coming down a Swiss mountain one October. Through an unfortunate combination of events, I was left alone with our three boys. The path became very narrow and it was getting dark. Being very steep both sides with slippery, dry grass, I put my 2-year-old on my shoulders, and held my 4-year-old's hand on the upper slope, while my 5-year-old walked steadily ahead. We sang some favourite songs and eventually came to a large meadow. The children knew we had lost our way but were not worried. It seemed like an adventure and I kept my adult fears to myself. Now it was very dark. Suddenly we walked into an electric fence and had difficulty getting through, but we managed and sang a not-minding-the-electric-fence song. The next thing was cowpats, but we made up a funny cowpat song. At last we reached a forest, and I had visions of a pine needle bed and twiggy blanket. Somehow being with the children kept my spirits up, for I knew I must be cheerful. Then, what a wonder and reward: the full moon came up and we could see where we were. Of course we sang 'I see the moon and the moon sees me . . .' Soon after, we saw a light, then a cottage so I knew there must be a track. Half an hour after that we met the frantic family search party, but we just kept singing and told them our story. I felt protected by an unseen force, and I know the singing helped keep us buoyant.

The older two remember this episode, and I think it was strengthening for us all. Later, we made a moving picture book about it, including a page with a moon we could push up.

Carolling or any singing round the neighbourhood is a joyful thing to do with friends and families. Singing in the car passes the time—more satisfying, I suggest, than listening to the radio or CD. Older children can sing rounds or songs with you, whilst little ones will join in anything. In a traffic jam, open the windows; others might join in. Singing can be a marvellous antidote to fear and boredom.

In summary

Children revel in imaginative play in the natural world, using all of Mother Nature's gifts. Such learning is a rich, rewarding, fulfilling experience. There is no need to entertain children who are used to such freedom; others will catch on if guided into this wonder-filled, un-planned, vital kind of childhood. In the next chapter we will see what kinds of simple equipment and playthings support such activity.

5
PLAYTHINGS, STRUCTURES AND TOOLS

For a Children's Garden

A place to sing and a place to play;
A place to build on a rainy day.
A space to dream and laugh and cry,
To skip and run, to chat and fly.
A place to hide, to climb and fall,
A world of beauty to charm us all.

Brooms for sweeping and dough for baking,
Bulbs to plant and leaves for raking.
A corner to muse and one to sow,
To dig and plant and watch things grow.
Nettles and prickles, insects and flowers;
Sun, wind and rain; frost, fog and showers.

How to keep rabbits out? And children in?
A post and rail fence, with wire dug in.
Grow roses all round, berberis, nasturtium,
Buddleia, forsythia, jasmine, viburnum;
Lavender, honeysuckle, herbs to store,
Japonica, periwinkle and much, much more.

Berries for birds and grubs for moles;
Colours and scents to nourish our souls.
We'll have clothes for all weathers, be allowed to take risks;
Cook with old saucepans, wooden spoons and sticks.
Live with earth and fire, water and air.
Have real bonfires (or not): a dragon's lair.

Chips and oak slabs, paving, and brick,
With benches of branches for parents to sit.
Willow and hazel stems growing apace
Weave houses and tunnels and archways and nests.
We'll have stories and picnics on logs and on planks,
Then move them around for pirates and pranks.

A house, a tunnel, a bridge and a wall,
A boat, a pond, a hill and a hole.
Lightness and dark, sunshine and shade,
Fruit trees too, and a veg patch made.
Steps, worms and insects, a hedge, mud and sand,
And a compost heap to feed the land.

A place to pile the logs up high
Or quietly watch the clouds go by.
To dream with the earth
And live under the sky.

By the author, 2002

Children of all ages will get the most out of structures and equipment which are as adaptable and non-representational as possible. It is amazing what children can invent with this kind of 'nothing'. The easiest and cheapest imagination-inspiring toys are those found in the abundant natural world, or objects which have been discarded.

Fallen tree . . . horse . . .

Special play place

Log for play

11 November. Chiu Shan will continue making the dolls' ladder with smaller fallen birch pieces and grass rope. *Review.* The children are copying, tying their own together.

Once my children found an enormous, stiff rope 4 inches thick and over 30 feet long washed up on the beach and insisted we stuff it into our small car. Another time they found large, heavy pieces of slate in a disused quarry, which we *had* to fit in amongst the camping equipment. They dragged an old ladder home, found in a pond, and all sorts of bits of wood. These things are still around and in use today. Children find the most surprising things *absolutely essential*, so it is really good if we can possibly satisfy their wishes, so long as they are not completely outrageous.

Children appreciate pine cones, leaves, rough stones and smooth pebbles, shells from local beaches and rivers, conkers and feathers. A bag or basket on walks holds these and other 'treasures' such as sycamore and ash keys, pine needles, twigs, rose hips, nuts, acorns and their cups, and chestnut cases. They can make awesome creatures from any of them. Parents may need patience to

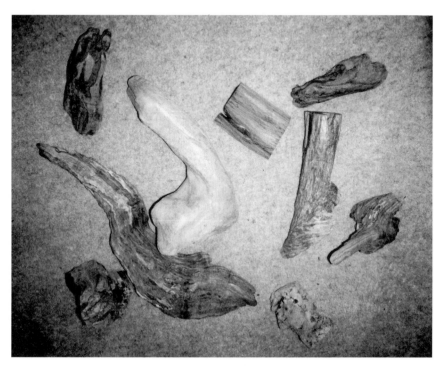

Nature's playthings

More toys

cope with these playthings, but small baskets or boxes for each sort helps. In the educational setting there can be particular places to store them. Naturally the family takes care to keep unsuitable objects out of reach of babies and toddlers. Fallen branches and other wood can be made into a variety of toys and equipment. Ask for waste wood from a tree surgeon or your local council.

> It is awe-inspiring for children to see people making things, engaged in real, archetypal processes. Home-made things are so individual, charming for the child to handle, full of life and love. One can make all sorts of things with little expertise. A bit of imagination, determination and practical ideas go a long way.

Equipment

Most of the following ideas work for any child up to at least 12 years.

Containers

Carts, wheelbarrows, buckets, crates, boxes, old prams and pushchairs are excellent for getting inside or loading up. A covered veranda is a good place to store playthings and equipment, and also good for babies and children to play or sleep outside even in the rain.

Girls like heavy things as well as boys

Table and chairs

Bricks, flower pots, logs, pieces of slate, planks or boards do well.

Tools for sandpit or earth play

If kept clean one collection for earth or sand is sufficient, otherwise a set for each. These are useful: trowel, spade, fork, rake, hoe, sieves, wooden spoons, saucepans, kettles and simple buckets. Old tennis, golf or other balls do for tunnels and castles to roll balls through and down. It is unnecessary to bring toys into the scene: the child's inspiration will make diggers, cars, people, etc. out of their treasures. Broken or cracked items should be mended or removed. Keep everything in a box or shed.

Scales

Coconut shell halves do well. The following sizes are only approximate; use what you have, preferably found outside. Take a 40 × 10 × 2 cm flat piece of wood for the base. Drill a hole in the centre to fit one end of a 40 cm long, 5 cm diameter branch. File the opposite end of this branch to a blunt point.

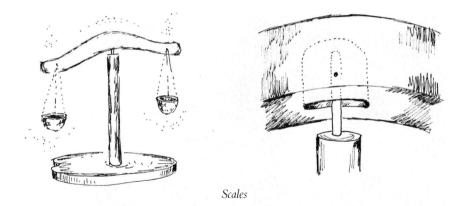

Scales

Glue it in. Drill 3 holes, spaced evenly apart, near the rim of each coconut shell. Thread 30 cm lengths of string through each and tie in a knot. Take a similar-sized branch to the vertical one and drill a hole either end to fit 3 strings each. Pass the 3 strings of each coconut through each hole evenly, tying them in a knot, or with a bead, the upper side. Make a hollow in the centre of the underside of this horizontal branch and balance it onto the blunt point of the vertical one. Children can adjust it when they play but you can put a nut and bolt through horizontally if you wish.

Xylophone or glockenspiel

Suspend pieces of wood or metal (could be metal tubes) from a tree or posts; hang a stick nearby to hit them. Test and tune them by sawing bits off.

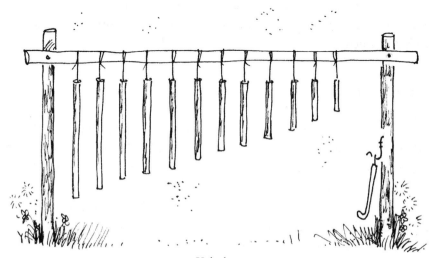

Xylophone

*Self-made
xylophone*

Thread string into earthenware flower pots, tie a twig, large button or hag-stone on, then hang them upside-down from a branch (out of the wind, or even a strong breeze may break them). Careful children can hit them gently with a wooden spoon.

'Treasure Island'

Intense activity and incentive arise from play with gutters, funnels, bits of metal, stones, boulders, bits of wood, logs, poles, branches, planks, card-board boxes (until rained on), crates, boards, shelves, bits of furniture, broken or whole bricks and tiles, string and rope, pots and pans, tyres, lad-ders, tree stumps and all such paraphernalia. Check for splinters and sharp edges. Old bicycle wheels make remarkable toys. Pipes are good for build-ing and for rolling balls down. A plumber or builder may have unneeded material.

Treasure Island

Tying, attaching

Ropes, cords and string are marvellous imagination and ingenuity-filling playthings. Of course you have to keep an eye on young children using them. Combined with cloths they make houses and camps. Pulleys on

At the workbench

ropes strung between and up walls, posts and trees or suspended over branches transport buckets, baskets, boxes, hoops... One likes to use natural rope but some becomes rigid when wet and rots. Soft synthetic rope in pretty colours, strong, rot and weatherproof, is available in sports shops.

Workbench, sawing horse, chopping block

Children and young people enjoy creating equipment and making firewood, obviously with an adult until responsible enough to work on

Everyone helps

their own. A large and small saw, rasps, files, screwdriver, screws and a drill are useful. Hammering just for the sake of it is not a very good image for the younger child.

In the 'kitchen'

Homely activities

Children like washing windows, tools and dolls' clothes, so need cloths, bowls, clothes pegs and washing line. They love beating or jumping on carpets and mats, and like needle and strong thread for threading peanuts for birds, sewing kit and fabric, boards, paper, scissors, paints, crayons and coloured pencils for painting, drawing and writing stories outdoors.

'Kitchen'

Tie three or more tall branches or poles together near the top to support a bucket hanging from the join.

Waterwheel

Waterwheel

Drill two 15 mm holes at right angles 2 cm apart through the middle of a small straight branch or dowelling about 5 cm in diameter. Push 2 pieces of dowelling about 50 cm long through them. Screw 4 paddles of rectangular boards, about 10 × 5 cm, to each end of the 2 pieces of dowelling. Support the ends of the branch either side of the stream on forked sticks pushed securely into the stream bed.

Boat

An old boat on dry land allows the imagination to travel. Upside down on strong, stable posts, it provides a roof. A dinghy on its stern, well supported, makes a great sheltered seat. Look in sailing clubs and local papers for an unwanted boat.

Sandpit

A sandpit may be the most popular outdoor place all year round in home or childcare setting. Children want to be right in it, rather than just play on the edge.

Deliciously soggy rain 'cooking'

Sandpits are cosy when bordered by flower beds or a low hedge with 2 or 3 small gaps; this helps stop running in and out and making the sand dirty. If sunk into the ground, a surrounding of brick, paving or wood at least 30 cm wide allows for sitting, sand modelling, 'cooking' and decorating. Sandpits need porous concrete or a porous membrane as a base, so the sand does not become muddy. If they are to be built on top of the ground, lay your base across and to the insides of a border of logs or boards. With appropriate warm and waterproof clothes, nothing should keep children out. Have small logs for sitting in cold weather. Different weathers present varied impressions: if dry, children sieve 'sugar'; if wet they can model; if frozen, digging is difficult; snow with sand makes fine puddings. Most sandpits need an anti-animal netting cover which children can remove and replace. Emptying footwear into the pit after play saves sand. Children can share in sweeping it back after play and giving a regular dig and rake over to keep it aerated and fresh. Removing leaves avoids rot. I suggest a minimum depth of 50 cm. A tree,

Canopy over sandpit with detail

hedge, wigwam, parasol or light tarpaulin gives sun and wind protection when necessary. Trowels, sieves, old saucepans, simple buckets, rakes and spades make satisfying tools.

Indoor sandpit

If you are brave enough, you can let your toddlers have sand under the kitchen table! We had a sandpit like this, and the children were happy, mostly staying in it. The simpler and more rhythmical their lives, the more likely this will be.

Cut a very large cardboard box (or two, endways on) with a Stanley or bread knife to about 30 cm high; cover it over with a large cloth. Plain blue or yellow is nice, to give the impression of a sandy beach by water! Fill it half-full with play grade sand, not builder's sand (that makes stains). Babies and young children are likely to play in it contentedly while you get on with your work. It is easy to sweep off the floor. You can do the same in a nursery if there is no opportunity for an outside sandpit.

For older children indoors, cut and stick cardboard boxes together to make a large, slightly irregular shape about 25 cm high with the tops cut a bit wavy. Put it on an old table which you have sawn the legs off to child height. Cover and fill as above.

Larger structures

Naturally these can be bought, but can be very expensive. There are companies using branches and reproducing natural forms in their equipment because they recognize their value. Rope structures of all shapes and sizes are exciting (see Appendix 2). **Much can be made at home or school.**

Some see-saws, animal and other shapes mounted on a large spring give children a fairly hyperactive experience rather than rhythmical movements. Slides, jungle gyms, trampolines, standard climbing frames and monkey bars afford opportunity for large motor development, yet their creative value is rather limited. A play ship may always seem like a ship; a log is just as serviceable and can also be a castle, a kitchen or a rocket. Another drawback to much standard equipment is that it removes the unpredictability found in nature, the differentiation in form and size which makes children more aware of what they are doing and how they need to use their body.

I recommend equipment made of wood rather than plastic or metal. Most hardwoods, e.g. chestnut, larch and oak, do not need treatment and last well. Please use native timber from sustainably managed forests. Several companies obtain timber from sustainable sources ('FSC': Forest Stewardship Council certified in the UK), and where necessary treat it with child and environmentally friendly preservatives which you can obtain for instance from some hardware stores, from Permaculture (see Appendix 2), wildlife magazines or the Internet.

Shelter

Children like to hide and get underneath things; they appreciate houses, bushes, small trees and hedges, where they can feel secure and be private.

Weeping trees are attractive for playing or eating underneath. Tie some branches together for a doorway or window. A rambler over a pergola or trellis provides shade or a tranquil corner. When dark, you can hang a lamp under it for a beautiful mood. Trellises fixed to posts at different angles or folded zig-zag make a beautiful roof in summer with wires or battens from one trellis top to the other. The died-back stems in winter give the feeling of shelter. You can make your own trellis with thin branches.

Wigwam

Drill small holes through the tops of several bamboo or other poles. Thread thin cord or string through the holes and tie together. Tie or peg blankets or cloths on. Pegging and tying things together helps children's spatial awareness, and can give them a sense of coordinating themselves.

Camps

Children up to adolescence love building dens, spaces to call their own. They need string, wire, a variety of wood, saw, drill and bits, screws and screwdriver, hammer and nails with perhaps a bit of adult expertise here and there, but they learn through trial and error and experimentation. Self-discovery is the best of teachers. As play spaces disappear under concrete and health-and-safety laws, young people are less and less able to do this. However, many without a garden are near a wood or common to build their second 'home'. They may need to ask for permission—and perhaps be refused—but in public woodland it is usually acceptable so long as only fallen wood is used, no damage is caused or litter left.

Christmas trees

Stand the tree (only natural ones!) outside afterwards, then feed the birds with apples, peanuts, cooked bacon rind, bunched stalks of millet and other grain hanging from it. Ask friends for theirs to 'plant' in the ground and make a little 'forest'. If they fall over, tie them one to another at their tops or fix with a stake.

Houses

Our kindergarten children enjoyed watching this house of recycled wood take shape. A clean and mended house will be loved and respected, and children are less likely to race in and out of it. Put an old-but-clean carpet in

Playhouse takes shape (my family)

Roof struts

Roofing felt

over builders' plastic to keep out damp, with cushions, saucepans, wooden spoons, etc. It will need occasional cleaning, but hauling it all out, shaking and sweeping it is fun. Afterwards the class or family can enjoy their next meal in the spic-and-span home. Children can remove their boots or shoes on the front step. Woolly socks keep feet warm. Windows and door can simply be spaces; if the roof is overhanging, curtains make it cosy enough. An

Roof nearly finished

Orange-box windmill + weather-vane on top

uneven or five- or six-sided house is fine. You might grow dog roses up the side, and build a bridge leading to it.

A house can be built with lopsided nooks and crannies on different levels, even around a tree. Such buildings can be made of recycled logs and have log seats inside. If you are digging up turf for building a playhouse, consider using it on the roof. A grassy roof with wild flowers is so pretty. Originally in the North they were laid on top of several layers of birch bark for insulation. Nowadays they are also laid on roofing felt. Playhouses can be low enough to crawl into, too small for grown-ups or just big enough to invite them to squeeze in for 'tea'.

8 January: Carry old carpet pieces to place between tree stump and old branch heap to stop weeds. Start making house next to it with smaller branches; push into ground (ideal now as so wet and soft) and weave left-over willow prunings through. Clear up rest of twigs for stick pile.

Children love straw-bale houses, and leaning bits and pieces of branch, planks and other wood onto a fence or wall and tying them together somehow. They like a den that can be frequently rebuilt. Branches and poles can be leant onto a cross-bar fixed between two posts sunk into the ground. As tying things up forms an important part of children's orientation development, give them thick string to bind everything together. Use tar-

Open-sided house

Frequently rebuilt house

Efficient den builder

Secret den

Woven den

Camp made with twisted grass string

paulins, old curtains, flags and cloths for extra cover. Using cloths to cover seats or branches lying on the ground makes great houses. All this encourages resourcefulness, ingenuity and physical development.

Tree houses

What is more glorious than to be up with the birds? Playhouses with an upper storey reached by a ladder give a superb feeling of height, but a house that does not even touch the ground is most special. It is of course essential to ensure it cannot fall down. With relevant precautions such as railings and walls, children can have a magical time up high.

Tree house

Tree house

My father built us a tree house up a lightning-struck oak over a pond. We could climb up inside the hollow as well as outside. Built of reclaimed materials, it was supported by one diagonal post from the house end to the bottom of the tree. It had a roof, half-height walls and a discarded church window at the end. Sometimes we slept in it. When my sister grew too big for the inside of the trunk, she got stuck, so we had to pull her out, like Winnie-the-Pooh.

You can climb into a tree house by ladder or rope ladder. If schools and early years' settings are lucky enough to have a tree, they can provide a tree house, as many people do not have a tree.

Willow structures

Willow can grow into wonderful structures. It is cheap, attractive, versatile, easy to grow and maintain and obtainable in various colours. It will regrow if broken; pruned twigs can be used for crafts.

(See Appendix 2 for planting details.) It is not necessary to make elaborate,

In the willow house

Children planting willow hedge with Mark

sophisticated shapes such as animals and castles. The more detailed and complicated, the less room there is for the child's own imagination. Clear weeds and lay cardboard, thick mulch or weed suppressant liner down so new plants can grow. Willow needs regular watering until established.

Their finished hedge

Newly sprouted willow

Nursery children preparing to plant a willow tunnel

Thereafter it is not fussy, despite being a plant of the waterside. Cuttings which do not take can provide archways, windows and doors. Weave new shoots in and out of each other. Hazel can be used too.

An old willow tree for climbing in our kindergarten garden was getting too big. Knowing it would sprout again, we cut all the branches off one winter about 3 feet above its heart. It looked sad for a year, but the children knew they would be able to climb in it again one day. We started weaving the new saplings into a large round 'nest'. A rope ladder of thick sticks and an old ladder found in a pond served for ascent. Gaps for windows appeared naturally. Where the branches had been cut off flat made places to stand and look out. The children still love their nest/castle/house/ship/kitchen . . .

Swinging and ropes

An archetypal plaything, swings can be fun, challenging or calming. Is it not the loveliest romantic thing under a tree? Some children like to go really high, while others just gently dream, as in a cradle.

3 November: Children tied string to the climbing ropes, using it to pull each other back and forth. They dragged logs behind the swings to get on as far back as possible.

Just a wide loop of thick rope or trapeze also makes a fine swing, or a rope with a knot or piece of wood tied at the bottom. 'Nest swings' for a small group are available. If woodchips or sand are used beneath, this naturally gets kicked out, so children can rake it back in again, thus making it last. You can drill holes through thick swing posts and thread ropes across for climbing and hanging. If two small trees are planted about 2 metres apart as a gift to a baby, some years later a beam can be put between them, resting in the nooks of two branches for a swing or rope.

Hammocks can hang from tree trunks or sturdy posts set in concrete with two diagonal supports each. Children can get over-enthusiastic about swinging each other rather than letting the one or two inside rock dreamily, so a gentle reminder may be necessary. *Ask an experienced person knowledgeable in physics to advise you on construction of swings, hammocks, tightropes and trapezes.*

A baby can lie in a Moses basket or other improvised cot with a hood, which you can hang from the branch of a tree. Fix four ropes securely to the corners or pass them right underneath. Ensure your attachment is safe and that the child is protected from the sun, then this will be a precious gift.

Tightropes encourage circus skills. Children can hold another rope above or practise with umbrellas. Hooked to or tied around posts or trees, ropes can criss-cross in any manner to invite numerous skills.

Trying things out

*Hammock for two
or more*

*Hammock as a
washing line*

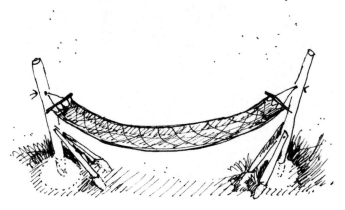

Hammock

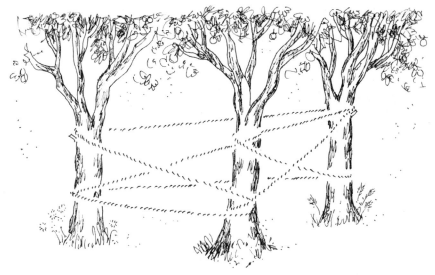

Ropes between trees

Getting messy and clearing up

Some children are lucky enough to spend blissful hours in old clothes mucking about outdoors, getting dirty and hungry. Adults who don't mind children getting in a mess are a blessing: you can always get cleaned

Time to tidy up

up again afterwards. Getting in a mess on purpose is a different matter, of course; then they may need a reminder that such behaviour is unacceptable.

It is really best if children learn to do as much clearing up as they can *on their own*. It is so easy to spoil them! From 4 or 5 years old they can tidy up increasingly independently, clean tools and put everything away every day. It is sensible to leave enough time and give everything a place. Tidying up can be made part of play. For instance, young children like to be 'rabbits', collecting the last little thing lying about. Sam hopped about putting tools away, saying, 'I'm a real rabbit.' Raking and sweeping whatever mess there is and making sure no dirt is carried indoors is part of the process.

> If tidying habits are begun very young, it should be no problem, especially if the adult is patient and does it too at first. This strengthens children's will-power and self-responsibilty, rather than the adult doing it all for them. It is important that tools, containers and playthings are looked after, cleaned and put away properly, even if they are 'only outside'. The image that a cared-for place gives the child goes very deep and helps to instil a morality in the soul which will later transform into love and respect for others and the world. It is also respectful to the child to ensure, for instance, that there are no worn-out or dirty playthings around.

In summary

Having the opportunity for unguided discovery allows children's innate resourcefulness and ingenuity to flourish. Problem-solving becomes natural in an environment uncluttered with pre-formed ideas or playthings. Here work and play are natural, rather than contrived for the sake of some learning objective. Let us offer our children a world of free play with simple toys and equipment where they can thrive and gain rosy cheeks and a warm heart. Living through the seasons outdoors in simple, imaginative ways gives health, joy and stability too (we will explore this further in the next chapter).

6
SEASONAL ACTIVITIES

Indoor and outdoor activities are often naturally connected. One obvious example is the 'bringing in' of a harvest, with all the cooking, bottling and preserving that can ensue. Seasonal, interrelated activity nourishes the whole child. The seasons are also naturally connected with seasonal celebrations marking stages in the year's cycle.★

Making lavender bags comes after growing and drying. Plants provide colours for dyeing. Pressed leaves embellish collages, mobiles, cards and lanterns. Seeds sown indoors are planted out later, some harvested and eaten indoors. Herbs are grown for cooking and teas. Fruit and vegetables can be washed, chopped and grated outside on a nice day. Tools are cleaned and put away under cover. Sheep's wool collected off fences makes original children's toys.† Pressed moss creates magical images and landscapes when stuck onto paper. Twigs, dried moss, leaves or flowers can be threaded through a loosely woven basket. Decorating with fresh flowers brightens every room. Make hanging mobiles with berries, twigs, pine needles, nuts, rose hips, leaves, pine cones, dried flowers, honesty pods, teasels and other seeds hanging from a branch.

At farmers' markets, fresh local produce is laid out in piles composed of attractive colours, shapes and smells. The Soil Association hopes to have every child visit an organic farm by the age of 11. They support year-round farm visits countrywide, to connect children with the earth and the food they eat.

General activities

Being among adults working in a positive mood helps to cultivate a good attitude to work, as something that is a privilege and a joy.

★ Please see Further Reading in Appendix 2 for books on celebrations.
† *Well, I Wonder*, see Further Reading in Appendix 2.

28 November. Walk to our house to see builders pulling out windows. Much interest, curiosity and questions.

30 November. Visit to see new windows. *Review.* Great deal of 'window replacement' during playtime this week.

Children love watching builders or any adult or older children's activity. In play they recreate the crane driver, chef, drain cleaner, road surfacer, combine harvester . . . On school sports day our kindergarten of 3–6-year-olds went to watch, taking a big ball, beanbags, skipping ropes and hoops 'to do it too' on the side. When they were older and saw all the 'sweet little children' on sports day, they looked back fondly to when they had been in kindergarten!

Children may enjoy a '(sea) shanty' to help little jobs along:

'Swish swish swish and tip tip tip, our brush and pan go flip flip flip.'
'Shoo shoo shoo shoo, scrub scrub scrub—whooooooooooooooooosh,
    rub-a dub.'
'Here we go, nice and slow, push the barrow, mind your toe.'

Children love sweeping if it is not seen as a chore. They happily spend ages pushing dirt and leaves about, aiming to get them in a pile. 'Sweeeeeee-Eeeep, Sweeeeeee-Eeeep, Puuuuuu-Uuuush, Sweeeeee-Eeeep.' Older children can discipline a temperamental pile better, although the wind may interfere.

Woodwork is a favourite activity. An old table can be substituted for a workbench. Children feel 'professional' in work apron or overalls. Tools must be of good quality and sharp, otherwise they are unsatisfactory and may slip. Potato peelers make good whittlers. Naturally sweeping up is part of the job. Children love sanding, even from the age of 2 (for 2 minutes!) and can also rub wood on sandpaper glued to a wooden block. A playgroup workbench was to be removed for resurfacing. 'Why not do it with the children?' I said. 'Someone could plane it, and the children help with the sanding and oiling.' 'The children are too young!' said the playgroup leader. 'Even your 3-year-olds will love to help,' I encouraged.

An outdoor bread oven for baking bread, pizzas, etc. is a wonderful thing. Children can follow the baking process right into their tummies. Wood preparation includes gathering dead sticks and branches. Children sort thicknesses for kindling and main burning, cut it to size with loppers or a saw and stack it correctly. The fire is made whilst dough is prepared, kneaded and left to rise. A few children are lucky enough to grow their own grain; others buy from a local farmer, threshing and grinding it with a hand mill.

Helping retrieve baked bread with bread-peel

Star-gazing

In chapter 4, I described lying on one's back and watching clouds; one can do this after dark too, even in urban places where they take on strange colours. Children are interested in astronomy. Young ones are filled with wonder at the light-filled stars or the moonlit night; later they like binoculars or a telescope, learning to recognize constellations.

The Big Bang and quantum physics are light years away from younger children, but by 11 or so they begin to take a scientific interest in such subjects.

Seasonal celebratory markers

With careful preparation of both children and event, open-air seasonal celebrations can make a joyful, deep impression. I will only mention a few here. There are so many different seasons and cultures around the world; you will naturally celebrate those closest to you. These are just ideas to set you going if it is new to you. And please don't forget to sing!

Children enjoy sharing in the food preparations and decorations. A sur-

prise prepared by an adult adds to the awe-inspiring moment. For instance:
after decorating the room, table or outdoor space for the celebration and just
before everyone gathers again, you might place a bowl of water in the centre
of the creations, with flower heads and lighted candles floating upon it, and
wound around with fine cloths and leaves. Decorations might be of furniture
covered with cloths, branches, nuts and other treasures from the natural
world, flowers, favourite dolls and anything else one might fancy.

Flower garlands are charming round the door. A branch can be hung up
with relevant seasonal things tied to it: paper birds, green and pink ribbons,

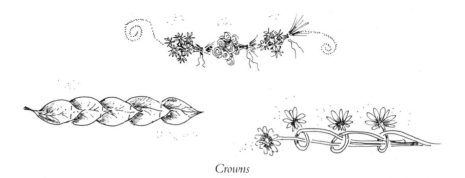

Crowns

Dandelion crown

tissue paper flowers, bundles of wheat . . . Make crowns with what is growing at the time: weave leaves and flowers into doubled, twisted string or raffia or run ribbon through and around twigs, flowers, berries, leaves and seeds. Decorated corrugated paper can hold twigs and stalks.

Birthdays

Birthdays have a special quality outside, amongst trees in the city park or little garden, in a field, on the beach or by a stream. Candles can be tricky outside, but can be protected by an umbrella. They can be pushed into sand or pebbles, along with flowers. We called sandwiches 'picnicwitches' on the beach so we didn't notice the sandy crunchiness so much. If the party is in the dark, children may like sparklers and lanterns.

Fireworks at celebrations

It has recently become more usual in the UK for people to enjoy fireworks at personally special times such as a party or wedding, rather than just around 5 November. However, many folks find them an unacceptable noise nuisance except on the latter occasion. Old people, small children, pets and wildlife suffer.

Beach birthday

Two inches are enough for fun

Ideas through the year

My focus here is on children in the British environment. Please adapt my suggestions to your own situations if you live in the Southern Hemisphere or other climates.

January

'It's coming out nice now,' winked an old man to me as snow fell from a grey sky. How children love the snow!

> *I like to think that long ago*
> *There fell to earth some flakes of snow,*
> *Which loved this cold grey world of ours*
> *So much, they stayed as snowdrop flowers.*

Mary Vivian

- Make a small igloo with large snowballs; put lanterns in it after dark.
- Slide on frozen puddles. Look through 'windows' of ice from them.
- Chop and saw wood. Mend wooden items on a dry day.
- Wash and tease your sheep's wool.
- Float snowdrops (or bell-shaped flowers any time) upturned on a bowl of water.
- Feed the birds, at least until the summer when the young have flown.

February

> *Look out! Look out!*
> *Jack Frost is about!*
> *He's after our fingers and toes;*
> *And all through the night,*
> *This gay little sprite*
> *Is working where nobody knows.*

He'll climb each tree,
So nimble is he,
His silvery powder he'll shake;
To windows he'll creep,
And while we're asleep,
Such wonderful pictures he'll make.

Across the grass
He'll merrily pass,
And change all its greenness to white;
Then home he will go,
And laugh, 'Ho! Ho! Ho!
'What fun I have had in the night!'

Cecily E. Pike

- Spring-clean the shed.
- Clean windows.
- Put dogwood and forsythia twigs in water for early flowering. Winter jasmine can be picked in December.
- Put up nesting boxes.
- Look for a scheme to join (see Appendix 2). Volunteers are needed in nature reserves. In the UK, the RSPB's 'Wildlife Explorers' and the Wildlife Trust's 'Watch' groups are specifically for the young.

March

March Wind

He huffs from the North
He puffs from the South.
He bulges his cheeks
And purses his mouth.

His swagger is cloaked
In blue of the sky.
He wears a white cloud
Tipped over an eye.

Author unknown

- Children help sieve and wheelbarrow compost around the garden.
- Enjoy pussy willow and catkins.

- Pick and chop young nettles for soup.
- Sow seeds in pots from now onwards.
- Make a scarecrow. Tie two sticks or stakes together in a cross, human-size, the upright one long enough to dig securely into the ground. Dress them in old clothes, stuffing them with straw, dry grass or other old materials (not paper as it goes soggy in the rain). Hair of straw or bits of wool, old boots, gloves and a hat are vital! Stuff fabric tightly for a head, e.g. old vest. Paint the face if you want, although conkers, potatoes, carrots and suchlike sewn on will do too. Give him a nice name and with any luck your new friend might keep some of the birds off.
- Cut newly sprouted herbs.
- Spring-clean paths, steps and terraces.
- Keep a bowl or aquarium for frogspawn, just three or four eggs so the tadpoles do not perish from lack of food and air. Take some weed and stones from the same pond as they eat the slime on them. A rock should stand out so the newborn frogs can climb out and breathe. Cover it then as they can jump (and if there are pets around). Return the tiny frogs to the same pond.
- Make a stick pile. Continually add to it for hedgehog homes, and for insects that thrive on rotting wood, so providing other wildlife nourishment.

April

Hark, the tiny cowslip bell
In the breeze is ringing,
Birds in every woodland dell
Songs of joy are singing.

Winter's o'er, Spring once more
Spreads abroad her golden store.
Hark, the tiny cowslip bell
In the breeze is ringing.

Spring has come to make us glad,
Let us give her greeting.
Winter days were cold and sad,
Winter's reign is fleeting.

Hearts are gay, blithe as May,
Dance and sing the lifelong day.
Spring has come to make us glad,
Let us give her greeting.

17th century

- Gorse flowers taste of coconut, a fine snack on a walk.
- Hang decorated eggs from a flowering bush at Easter.
- Children can take pretty baskets to collect the eggs they find, which the Easter Hare has hidden in grassy nests.
- Children enjoy standing under a fruit tree with petals falling over them, either naturally or through gentle shaking. They also like having a 'shower' under a tree if you shake the branches gently after rain, or being covered with snow in the same way in winter.
- For a miniature garden, fill a plate with earth, then moss, stones, twig 'trees' and early flowers. Keep it damp. Make a little river between the moss, and a bridge of bark.
- Fill eggshell halves with earth and quick-growing seeds. Make a hole in the bottom for drainage.
- Look for birds' nests and the source of babies' cheeps. (Children must not disturb the birds or they will desert their young.)
- Tadpoles hatch and wiggle in the pond (also food for dragonfly larvae amongst other things).

May

There piped a piper in the wood
Strange music—soft and sweet—
And all the little wild things
Came hurrying to his feet.

They sat around him on the grass,
Enchanted, unafraid,
And listened, as with shining eyes
Sweet melodies he made.

The wood grew green, and flowers sprang up,
The birds began to sing;
For the music it was magic,
And the piper's name was—Spring!

E.L. Marsh

In Britain, many Morris dancers welcome the sunrise on 1 May with their flying ribbons, bells, sticks and music. Take a thermos, sandwiches, rug and warm clothes. Other countries have their own dawn celebrations.

3 May: Take ladder and maypole ribbons to oak tree and tie to branch. *Review*: Great fun, not much wind.

13 May: (We now had a proper pole.) Wrap pale green crepe paper and crepe flowers round maypole. Make crown for top with fresh flowers on wire ring.

Maypole dancing is a lovely activity. You may have to do it in raincoats or hang onto the wind-blown ribbons, ending up in a glorious coloured knot! It is nice to prepare by dancing every day for two or three weeks, maybe indoors with ribbons tied to the ceiling, before parents come to watch. Parents and practitioners can make live music on recorders, tambourine, accordion, fiddle, guitar, drum or whatever is around. There are books of maypole and other folk tunes which your library, music or bookshop will have. Families can dance round their maypole too; invite friends round and make music or just sing. It does not have to be sophisticated—that is part of the fun. Children enjoy decorating the maypole and making flower crowns (thread flowers and leaves through plaited raffia or string). There are plenty of wild flowers by the wayside in city and country now, so it is no problem for children without a garden. Even boys of 8 are happy to wear a flower crown if they have not been told it is 'sissy'. More demanding maypole dances, for children from about 8 upwards, involve complex interweaving of the ribbons and much focused concentration . . .

- Stand under may (hawthorn) trees for a snow-blossom covering.
- Children love daisy and dandelion chains, and you can also make crowns with these.
- Slide fallen rhododendron flower centres over a twig.
- Watch tiny frogs appear.
- If celebrating the Whitsun festival you may like to use flowers of the Compositae family (daisies, dandelions, etc.). Because these blossoms are 'composed' of many separate 'individuals' creating a whole flower in harmony together, they can represent human beings strengthened by a divine source reaching out to each other in friendship and understanding.
- For hay fever sufferers: limit activity outside; shut bedroom windows during the day and open at night, close again in the morning when pollen concentration is at its highest; avoid the car's fan and air-conditioner;

wash pollen out of hair before bed; dry clothes indoors; take clothes off outside bedroom and leave them there; avoid cigarette smoke.

- Wake the family early to hear the dawn chorus, best in woods. Have a special breakfast afterwards. Local bird groups know where to hear particular birds in your part of the world.
- Watch bats and swifts at dusk, swooping about at high speed.

June

- Wash dolls' clothes and bedding.
- Use dandelion clocks to tell the time; catch the seeds for fun as they blow away.
- Press moss for pictures. Spread out gathered moss as flat as possible in between several layers of absorbent paper. Press under a heavy weight, e.g. a pile of books, or in a flower press. Leave for a couple of weeks. When dry, gently arrange pieces of the moss on clean paper and stick down with white glue to make a wonderful landscape. For protection, put the picture in a picture frame behind glass or hard plastic. Take care not to gather more moss than necessary.
- Hang small bunches of lavender and herbs (or lay them out) to dry, out of sunlight.
- Moth balls: make bunches of thyme, lavender and rosemary.
- Bouquet garni: tie mixed dried herbs into small muslin bags for soups and stews.
- Pot pourri: mix dried, sweet-smelling flowers and herbs to put in a bowl.
- Herb tea: infuse certain herbs/flowers/fruits for about 2–5 minutes. Properties and infusion times for each type vary: please refer to books. Only use those you know to be safe. The most common are easily available. Many are used medicinally. Use *unsprayed*, preferably organic, fresh or dried ingredients. Single herbs are especially good for young children with their delicate, developing taste. Try mixing two or more for older children. For an especially delicious one, combine some or all of these: finely chopped organic orange and lemon peel; rose hips; lime flowers; apple or other mint; young birch, blackberry and raspberry leaves; calendula flowers.
- Play the 'smells game' with children over 5 or 6: blindfold one child at a time, gently crush herb leaves in your hand and hold under child's nose. Can they tell which flower or herb is which?

- Thin out carrots to nibble.
- Flowers are best picked early in the day when they are at their most fresh and strong, refreshed from sleep as it were, like people. The early morning sun is important for plants too.
- Make elderflower syrup (see recipe books or *Family, Festivals and Food* in Appendix 2).
- Borage, nasturtium and other edible flowers are pretty in salads.
- Make thin sandwiches of bread, butter and (unsprayed) rose petals.
- Pudding: form strained yoghurt mixed with fruit pieces into a cone in a glass bowl. Stick the heart-shaped (unsprayed) rose petals to the mixture, and to the sides of the bowl with water. Decorate a cake with the petals.
- Make flower and leaf presses: drill a hole at the corners of two sanded boards, 20 × 30 cm for butterfly bolts. Lay petals and leaves between them in layers of absorbent paper. Leave for two weeks. For cards or pictures, stick the flowers and leaves on with white glue.
- Midsummer is the time for making merry: simple music in songs and dancing, games, plays, parties, picnics. Choose stories and songs about bees, sun, fairies and fireflies.
- Honey is a sun-filled food. *It is thought there may be a risk for infants. Consult your health visitor or other medical practitioner if you are uncertain.*

Elderflowers for juice

- 'Bees': wrap a piece of yellow wool three times round tiny alder or other cones, slightly apart, catching a tiny piece of net or gold paper in the middle for wings. Hang them by thread on a stick for the children to fly.
- This is a special time to invite parents for a bring-and-share class picnic.
- Some celebrate the St John's Tide. A festival fire symbolizes the chance for new growth and change: the phoenix rising from the ashes, overcoming one's difficulties.

Drawing Midsummer pictures in the sand

July

> *Lavender's blue, dilly, dilly, Lavender's green,*
> *I shall be king, dilly, dilly, you shall be queen.*
>
> *Call up your men, dilly, dilly, set them to work,*
> *Some to the plough, dilly dilly, some to the cart.*
>
> *Some to make hay, dilly dilly, some to cut corn,*
> *While you and I, dilly dilly, keep ourselves warm.*

Old rhyme

- Children help carting mulch (fresh or half-rotted plant material) to plants to preserve moisture.
- Hollow out thick elder stems for skipping rope handles. Round off the ends with file and sandpaper. Make a plaited or twisted rope with thick knitting cotton and pull it through the hollow stems. Make a knot at each end.
- When clematis, jasmine and other clinging plants have finished flowering, cut them back and use the pieces to weave crowns. Thread flowers into them or make little baskets. Willow is good for this too.
- Make lace leaves by gently tearing away the skin to leave the veins. Horse

Willow crowns

chestnut leaves are good for this. Sometimes you can find a magic leaf from the year before, which has formed itself into lace.

- Fill a bag of soft material (about 20 × 30 cm) with dried cherry stones. Warm them in a low oven in winter for a 'hot water bottle'. Or fill a bag with millet or wheat grain (preferably organic), and add dried lavender, then warm up.
- Hang poppy seed heads upside down for 'bell' decorations.
- Peel honesty seed pods for play or decorations.

August

- Phosphorescence surrounds (good) swimmers in the sea at night: fantastic!
- Go exploring in the holidays to local places you have not been before.
- Stay up late to watch for shooting stars from now through the autumn.
- Pick wild fruits away from traffic (avoiding toxins).
- Ask a farmer if you may harvest a few grain stalks for threshing or decorations.
- Dry the straw for straw stars at Christmas.
- Pick first blackberries. Best eaten at the bush, but if enough to take home, leave spread out on a tray first to collect any maggots, as they make their way to the top.

- Watch birds enjoying elderberries, and pick some. You may have other kinds of wild berry near you.
- Pick up apple, pear, plum and other windfall fruits, your own or of neighbours who do not want them. Many people do not bother nowadays, which seems wasteful. Wear thick gloves if wasps are about.
- Pick early apples and pears if you have them, or from neighbours who do not want theirs. For keeping, wrap individually in used, clean paper (tissue paper is good), and store on trays or shelves in a cool place. Check weekly for rotten ones; put on compost heap.
- Put a cat net over baby's pram in the garden at any time of the year if there are cats about, but it will protect against wasps and other insects in summer and autumn too. Ensure there are no gaps.

September

'What hue shall my apples be?'
Asked the little apple tree.
'That is easy to decide,
Have them green,' the grasses cried.
But the crimson roses said,
'We should like to have them red.'
While the dandelion confessed,
Yellow seemed to them the best.

When the apples all were ripe,
Many wore a yellow stripe.
Some were red and some were seen
Dressed in coats of softest green.

Leo Burns

- Preserving food: drying, bottling, freezing, making jams, jellies and syrups of wild and cultivated fruit and vegetables. Farm shops and farmers' markets will have ingredients you lack. Ask if you can gather (unsprayed) windfall fruit.
- Crab apples, widely found in the wild, make beautiful jelly, also with haws from the hawthorn tree. Use apples for pie, jelly, crumble, cake, juice.
- Make pretty labels for herbs, jams and juice; decorate tops with fabric circles.

- Make blackberry crumble and jam, delicious if mixed with apples.
- Use elderberries for jam, jelly or pie mixed with blackberries, or make syrup for coughs (see recipe books and *Families, Festivals and Food* in Appendix 2).
- Cover beans (also apple pieces) with a cloth and dry in an airing cupboard or slow oven. Keep in an airtight container. Soak the beans in winter for stews. Eat the apple pieces on walks. String up cored apple rings to dry in a clean, airy place. Organic apples do not need to be peeled.

12 September: Apple juicing in press. Cut out 'bad' bits for compost heap, chop, grate in hand grater, press, drink for break.

17 September: More apple-juicing. Children watch bottling at a distance (danger from very hot water, see below).

- To preserve juice, wash, rinse and keep glass bottles in very hot water until filling. Boil ladle, funnel and tops (from wine-making shop). Bring juice to 75°C, fill bottles to the brim, push tops in and lean upside down until cool.
- Children enjoy the Harvest Festival. Some observe Michaelmas, a celebration of inner strength: the summation of summer's light and heat to kindle courage, resilience and awareness during the dark months to come.

Bake a harvest or dragon loaf with the children. Use your favourite bread recipe, or one from a bread book. Soak whole grains overnight to add to the dough.

For the *harvest loaf*, first make a big, flat shape of two thirds of the dough; put it on a greased baking tray. Cover it with the following, made of the rest of the dough: a 'sheaf of corn' tied with 'string': children love rolling out long 'worms' for 'corn stalks' and 'string'; 'ears of corn' are made of small oblongs snipped (not wholly cut) along their length with scissors (extra fun); 'hedgehogs' are made in the same way but the oblongs are fatter; 'mice' on top of the sheaf are rounded oblongs with 'ears' and 'nose' pinched out and another 'worm' for a 'tail'.

Children also enjoy making *dragon bread* for Michaelmas. Let your imagination fly as you form the dough into a dragon shape on a baking tray and snip it with scissors as above. Add feet (two, six, more...) and maybe a few extra heads. Push in dried fruit and seeds for eyes and additional decoration.

October

- Collect conkers, beechnuts and hazelnuts for play. Keep out of reach of toddlers.
- Make (flat) conker dragons to pull along the floor: skewer holes and thread string through decreasing sizes of conkers; this forms head, body and tail; tie legs of two strings of conkers onto the body in appropriate places.
- Crack ripened nutshells with a hammer (fun). Jump on prickly sweet chestnut cases, or open them with strong gloves. Slit the shell before roasting to avoid an explosion.

> *10 October.* Expedition day. Pick up chestnuts. Picnic under tree.
>
> *11 October.* Cut and roast chestnuts for break.

- Plant bulbs from now onwards.
- Fungi erupt in grass and forest. Seek an expert before experimenting with either tasting or cooking. See evidence of animals in the nibbles. From the age of 4, children can generally be trusted not to eat anything they should not.
- Pumpkin house: cut out a roof, hollow out the pumpkin, cut doors, windows and chimney hole. Use things from nature inside as 'furniture', 'carpet' and 'people'. A night-light inside roasts the roof: delicious smell! When the children are asleep, squeeze it into the fridge or cover and leave it outdoors so it lasts several days. Dry and roast the seeds for salads or a necklace.
- Hollow out small pumpkins or turnips for lanterns; shave off the skin in shapes or patterns with a potato peeler or sharp knife. Place a nightlight inside. Thread wire through to carry or hang up.
- Catch falling leaves; roll in their windswept piles. Rake them for leaf mould, continuing all winter if there are a lot.

Bulb planting

Leaf raking

November

> *One misty, moisty morning, when cloudy was the weather,*
> *There I met an old man, clothed all in leather.*
> *Clothed all in leather, with a cap under his chin,*
> *How do you do, and how do you do, and how do you do again.*

Old rhyme

6 November: Collect leaves of all shapes and colours in basket on walk. Press under carpet in hallway between layers of paper. Enjoy walking and jumping about on carpet for next two weeks. Use for transparencies, cards and mobiles.

- Children enjoy 'carving' a rotten piece of wood with an old spoon, blunt knife or another piece of wood.
- Select a fat pine cone. Sew a head (bead) on. Leaving an uncovered 'face', stitch a cloak of fabric onto the 'body' and 'head'.
- Now is another time for gathering strength for the dark and cold of winter. Many celebrate Martinmas, Divali or other light-bringing festivals in the dark, singing and guided by lanterns, with a hot drink and special

Preparation for lantern festival

bread or buns. Wind and rain make this festival even more poignant and memorable so long as the adults are undaunted. Sometimes it is a quiet, beautiful night under a full moon.

December

- Rose hips ripen after frost; if straight off the bush, turn them inside out to remove the pips. Chop and dry them for tea infusions. Make jam (use more water than normal), sieving out the pips and bristles.

8 December: Picked dog rose hips. Chopped fresh rose hips for tea on picnic by rose bush. Pink, sweet, delicious.

- Pick sloes (blackthorn) with gloves, also after frost, for syrup: fortifying; good for colds.
- Some like to mark the four weeks of Advent as a gradual preparation for Christmas.

28 November: The children were enthusiastic about our preparations for Advent (tidying, cleaning, washing, polishing, sweeping outside, cleaning every last leaf from the sandpit then raking it). They made a huge 'Advent sandcastle', excitedly scraping the bottom of the pit ('to Australia').

- Children can help cut and make small bunches of pine twigs for a big wreath, and make their own little rings. The pine is fragrant, and sticky resin is also a sensory experience. Twist August-harvested straw, wrapped with string, into a ring to hang for decorations.
- Make straw stars from the harvested straw (see craft books).
- Fold a pliable twig five or six times in and out of itself for a star.
- Our family has a tradition of collecting a Christmas midday picnic from what is around in the house. When the children were young I slipped fruit into my pocket as a balance to their choices. We go for a long walk, and the picnic takes place wherever we like. On the whole we have been blessed with good weather. Our special meal is in the evening when we are really hungry.

Gifts

Details for many of these can be found in the calendar pages above.

Made by children:

Leaf necklace: thread string through 2 holes in each leaf.

Crown or similarly made necklace

Funny creature: push pine needles, beechnuts, leaves etc. around a pine cone or make one from fruit, vegetables, nut cases, twigs, etc.

Dew drops: thread small pearly beads onto about 50–80 cm lengths of stiff pointed grass (they should sit near the top). Put in a vase.

Miniature garden

Lavender bag

Pot pourri

Bouquet garni

Moth balls

Vegetables, flowers, fruit, herbs, fruit salad, vegetable soup (from own garden)

Seedlings

Sprouted cress or other edible seeds

Sprouting bulbs

Home-made jam, chutney, jelly or juice

Wrap presents in self-decorated paper or ironed, reused gift paper, tied with twisted cotton or woollen yarn.

For a child who is happy with simple things (ever fewer, although they may slowly begin to appreciate them):

Hiking boots, thick socks, hat, rain gear

Rucksack, bag, basket, box for treasures

Light-weight binoculars, magnifying glass, compass

Gardening, workshop or sandpit tools, sandpaper

Work gloves, apron, overalls

Workbench

Broom, scrubbing brush, watering can, jug, bucket

Wheelbarrow, trolley, cart

Small cupboard, box or shed for tools

Swing, seesaw, rope ladder, ladder

Skipping rope, rope, string, pulley, ball, hoop, kite, windsock, windmill

Paper, bark or wooden boat

Hobbyhorse, play reins

Fishing net, fishing tackle

Tarpaulin, cloths, wigwam

Treasure Island items: see chapter 5

Large branch or plank (the latter can be sanded and polished) for climbing, small ones for building

Bench

Bat box, bird table or feeder, bird bath, nest box, bird food

Bulbs, seed packets, seedlings

Plants, tree

Bus or train tickets (for the family)

Token towards possible membership of a conservation or wildlife youth group.

For a baby, for the future:

Bulbs, tree, shrub

Games

Lack of space or facilities can be overcome by imagination. One could link games for a party with the elements (see below). We have enjoyed the following selection of games in family, kindergarten and school. Singing games were once the life-blood of children's communities. Full of wit, wisdom, sociability, fun and rhythms, they help heart, brain, limbs and lungs to breathe and flourish. See *Children's Games* in **Further Reading** or ask in your library if you do not have any up your sleeve.

Catching

> 'I don't want you to be the wolf,' said Annie, 4. 'You can be the wolf with me and we'll take care of each other,' I said, needing to start the game by being the 'wolf'. She was happy with that. In general young children don't like being isolated from the group as a single 'character', but it's OK with someone else . . .

'What's the time Mr Wolf?' everyone calls, some way behind the wolf. '3 o'clock,' says the wolf (any time but 12). Children take three strides forward, the aim being to reach him before he turns round to catch them. 'What's the time Mr Wolf?' '6 o'clock.' six strides. 'What's the time Mr Wolf?' '12 o'clock, dinner time!' Mr Wolf turns to catch a hapless 'victim' who now becomes the wolf.

Fox and Hen: 'Hen' faces 'chicks' a few yards off, singing: 'All my children come to me!' Chicks: 'We dare not!' Hen: 'Why not?' Chicks: 'Because of the fox not.' Hen: 'All my children come to me!' Fox at the side runs in and tries to catch a chick as they rush to the hen. The caught chick becomes the fox. With children under 6 there can be several hens and foxes; one does not need to ask what they want to be.

> When I needed my kindergarten group to come together at an unusual time I sang, 'All my children come to me!' and, remembering this game, they came.

Tag: A hopping 'rabbit' touches someone who becomes another rabbit. They each 'catch' another so there are four hopping rabbits and so on. Try playing with flying birds, crawling beetles or jumping lambs.

Cat and Mouse: Children hold hands in a circle, guarding the 'Mouse' inside it, and attempting to keep the 'Cat' out by lowering or raising arms.

Grandmother's Footsteps: 'Grandmother' stands some yards away from the group, facing away. The children creep towards her. She turns, declaring the names of those she saw moving. They have to return to the beginning (cries of 'I wasn't! You did! It's not fair!'). But grandmothers have ultimate authority whether they are 4 or 84. The one who manages to touch her becomes the next authoritarian grandmother.

> 'Again!'—'Again?'—'Again!' Mummy and her 18-month-old ran after Daddy again round the big beds of plants. 'Where's Daddy?' said Mummy, as they stopped and looked into the tall bushes. He appeared to much laughter, then ran off again only to reappear to catch his son then run off once more. 'Again!'—'*Again?*'—'Again!'

Hiding and hunting

> 'Just don't go near the stinging nettles again!' said Mum playing hide-and-seek. How children love hiding, as an inner identification with a private place. So they build dens and have secrets. Yet they need to be discovered and acknowledged! My assistant once went to hide behind a tree with bushes all around while the children followed out of imitation. He slipped from one place to another, children behind, while I pretended to try and find them. 'We're like robbers,' said one child. This kind of game is so exciting, whether with 30 children or in the family.

Little Tree Says: Everyone hides behind a tree, bush or other large object. A catcher sings: 'Little tree says, "run to me"'; all change places while catcher touches one, who becomes catcher. They like the suspense of the catcher hesitating then speeding up, e.g. 'Little ... tree .... says .... "run .... to me".' Under 6 years, a catcher is unnecessary—they just enjoy changing places.

Sardines: One hides, finders stay with hider, the space becoming increasingly squashed.

Hunt the ...: Someone hides an object, others seek it with 'warm ...... colder ... warmer ... hot! The younger the child, the larger and more visible it needs to be.

Scavenger Hunt: Children find objects on a list, for example: black feather, prickle, nail, etc. Non-portable variation to tick off: hole in tree, blue tit, red car...

Blindfold: For over 6-year-olds, in pairs. One leads a blindfolded child to touch bark, leaves, prickles (gently!), water, etc., guessing what it is. This is a small indication of what it is to be blind.

Wolf: My children adored an old friend who used to play 'Wolf' with them. He ran ahead and hid, leaping out of the bushes to chase them when they crept furtively by. This game lasted for a mile or more.

Copying

Follow my Leader: If children are cold, make up fast movements.

Adventure: For children over 7, sitting in a circle. The narrator relates an adventure, making appropriate noises and gestures with hands, knees, feet and voice, while all copy, e.g. '. . . They came to a swing bridge and wobbled over it . . . a lion approached . . . they ran up a tree . . .' etc.

Where to? For children under 8. The adult says: 'Where shall we go today?' Adult (or children when they know the game) says: 'To Anywhere!' Adult marches off in little circles round a tree, back up, down again or whatever, followed by children in a loose line or group. 'Where shall we go now?'— 'To Nowhere!' Go off again, backwards on heels, hopping round or whatever. Repeat with 'To Somewhere', walking in funny ways, running off, suddenly stopping . . .

Races (two of so many)

Cart or boat game: Tie string 3–8 metres long to bark, a toy boat, cart or lorry with a small gift in each (e.g. strawberry, dried apricot, balloon). Young children wind it up slowly round a stick or skittle; older children have a race, winding it onto a cotton reel.

Snail race: Put two snails a couple of feet away from a lettuce leaf. They may go astray and have to be put back on track.

Observation

Hunt the difference: A family game for a walk, with a book for identification. How many different plants can you see? Points are unnecessary. You can make variations, such as: autumn colours (terracotta, browns, oranges, yellows, golds, pinks, reds); a hedgerow with sweet chestnut, oak, blackberry, bryony, blackthorn, hazel, hawthorn, bracken, gorse, ling, bell heather . . .

Circumferences: How many people does it take to stretch round a big (or thin) tree trunk?

I Spy: Use every letter of the alphabet in turn, such as ant, bee, church, dusk. For pre-literate children use the sound of the letter rather than its name, e.g. 'Buh' not B, or use colours.

Pubs, churches: To combat boredom in the car, children can play the pub/church/garage/silver car (or whatever) game. Everyone chooses some object and gets a point for each sighting.

Bike Ride Memory: Look at the map and work out the next few miles; then make up rhythms to avoid stopping to look again, e.g. 'Left, right, left'— 'Straight-on, straight-on, right.'

Balance

Obstacle course/circus: Use chairs, bricks, clothes-horses, hoops, stepping stones, logs, cardboard boxes, ropes for under, over, round, through, pulling, hopping, crawling...

Sensitive feet: Fill boxes with different materials to walk on in bare feet: grass cuttings, pebbles, sand, conkers, acorns, leaves, wood chips, soil, shavings, wet mud etc.

Stilts: Pierce a hole in the tops of two tins; thread about 1.5 m thick string through each to make loops. Stand on the tins holding the string. Alternatively, saw two pieces of wood or log about 15 × 15 cm; attach string to either side of the top of each.

Rolling: Guide hoops, wheels, tyres, logs, barrels or big pipes through an arch or gate.

Jumping and skipping

Skip with long or short ropes; use walls, straw bales, stumps, mounds and planks at varying heights for jumping off or between. Sung or spoken chants help rope and children go round.

> *Blue bells, dummie dummie shells,*
> *Evie, Ivy, O—ver.*
> *Charlie Chaplin★ went to France*
> *To teach the ladies how to dance.*
> *First your heel and then your toe*
> *Then ye do Big Birlie-O.*
> *Big—Birl—lie—O!*

Old rhyme, Scotland

Two people hold a long jump rope for others to skip or jump over: *Snakes* (wiggling it on the ground, others jump out of the way); *Waves* (shaking it up and down); *High Jump* (holding it at different heights, depending on the age/ability); *Sways* (waving it from side to side); *Run-throughs* (run from where the

---

★Or other name such as yours or the children's.

rope comes towards you), and finally jumping within the turning rope. As soon as children can jump, they can do all the first four, obviously gently at first, becoming increasingly challenging. From 6 or 7 they can do the other two.

Throwing and rolling

Frisbees, boomerangs, boule, volleyball, beanbags, pétanque, quoits, hoops. Choose balls of varying sizes and materials according to children's ages. Tightly rolled (unwanted) cloth bound with string, or a rolled-up-sock, does as an unsophisticated ball.

> *Onesome, twosome, I'll go to Sea,*
> *Bailbunky, hamaladdie, weather read-y.*
> *Sipsop, sipsop, sipsop, hen,*
> *Pennywise, crosswise, three fine men.*
> *If I had a cockerel, I'd call him Lou,*
> *I'd teach him how to Cock-a-doodle Doo.*
> *If I had a hen, I'd call her Meg,*
> *I'd count every time she laid an egg.*

Old rhyme

Rhymes help balls bounce on the ground or wall, or throwing quoits, beanbags and balls to one another. Throwing one through a hoop while someone rolls the hoop along is tricky. Children make up innumerable games with hoops if left to their own devices!

> *Plainie, Clappie, Rolling Pin.*
> *To bacKie, Right hand, Left hand*
> *High si-Toosh, Low si-Toosh.*
> *TelePhone The Answer,*
> *Touch my Heel, Touch my Toe,*
> *Through ye Go, big Birly-O.*

Old rhyme, Scotland

Tunnel: Everyone stands in a column, legs apart; the one in front throws a ball through this 'tunnel'. The one at the end runs to the front and repeats the exercise. Harder than it sounds! From 5 years.
Odds and Evens: In a circle of an uneven number: throw the ball over the top of the next person to their neighbour. From 6 years.

Catch-a-Name: Throw something in the air and call out a name; that person catches it. From 5 years.

Hoop and ball: Hang a hoop from a suitable place, tie a bell to the top and throw balls through to hit it. From 3 years.

Markers: Rolled-up jumpers or sticks do for goalposts, bases or stumps. A small board or thick stick serves as a bat. Unsophisticated ball as above.

Fishing

Make fishing rods of a stick with string and wire bent into a hook at the end. Spread out a blue cloth ('water') bunched up for 'waves'. 'Fish' are little parcels of dried or fresh fruit wrapped in tissue paper with a wire loop attached, or pairs of cherries.

The elements

The four elements of earth, water, air and fire are also recognized in the four seasons (outside the tropics).

The beach, feeling earth and water elements

Mud pit

Earth (winter)

Here is the mineral, physical element. Many children love playing with mud, stones, puddles, ditches, mole tunnels and icicles. They like building with old bricks using 'mortar' of mud, or laying paving or a path. They like mixing mud cement and smoothing it with an old, flat trowel, maybe 'mending cracks' they find in a wall or a path. 'Jack Frost' forms his artistry on cars and windows with single glazing. Hoar frost on trees is unforgettable. Children enjoy collecting quartz crystals from paths and beaches, and sand sparkles in sunshine. The gnome, elemental creature of the earth, lives underground.

Earth games

Pictures in the sand: If the sandpit is dug over, brushed and combed with a rake, eager fingers can draw pictures. Streamers (a strong twig with crepe paper strips or ribbons tied at one end) can be stood in it for hoopla. Make hoopla rings for throwing over the sticks by twisting pliable twigs together (e.g. birch, clematis, jasmine, willow, prunings of clinging plants); 20 cm diameter is suitable for under-5s, 15 cm for under-8s, 10 cm over 8s (the smaller the more difficult).

Shooting Stars: Stitch small cloth bags, fill them with sand, tie them up with long ribbons. Throw them into baskets arranged at different heights on boxes, stools, chairs and tables.

Birds in the Nest: Each person takes 10 small stones. Someone puts some into one hand and asks the next person, 'How many birds in the nest?' If correct, they receive those. If wrong, they give the same number up. Simple arithmetic required; when more than three or four people play, higher mathematics. For any age, starting as soon as children can count properly, with four or five stones at first.

Aiming: Hit a tin-can or breakwater with stones.

Pebble or Rock Castles: Build these on the beach; more difficult than sand. Wide walls are needed at the base.

Newton Effect: Place two bricks/stones/blocks of wood on a flat surface, end on. Hold one and hit it with a third. The front one shoots away. Experiment with different and more objects. Any age from about 4.

Nine Men's Morris, Mill or Merrills: This ancient game can be marked out with twigs or chalk or scratched into the ground. The 'men' can be stones. It has been found, for instance, scratched onto old Chinese, Egyptian and Etruscan floors and low walls. The rules can be found on the Internet.

Noughts and Crosses: Mark this out as above; use stones for noughts and sticks for crosses.

Snow pictures: An adult or older child shuffles along in a spiral with everyone following, thereby naturally squeezing closer and closer together. The leader turns and all shuffle out again. You can make any shaped trails like this. Children love to make 'angels' or 'butterflies' by lying down and spreading their arms and legs out and back again.

Water (spring)

Spring is the time of new life and growth; without water nothing can grow. Blood flowing is a watery, life force. There is water at the end and beginning of life. The water elemental is the 'water sprite' or 'undine', portrayed for example in the ballet *Giselle*. Many old stories tell of healing arising through some water-related activity, like 'The Water of Life' from Grimm's fairy tales. Playing with water is important for children, especially for the nervous child. The human body is 70 per cent water, and we feel an affinity with it, at ease, especially children. It is therapeutic for children to play in warm coloured water (add a couple of drops from a tube of watercolour). Although much water today does not have the curative properties one could wish for ('Mummy says you mustn't eat ice, it's got pollution in it'), nonetheless water is a healing force. Dew, a stream, puddles, mud, dripping gutters, snow, clouds, rain, mist and the rainbow: all are gifts for children, as are words like swishing, swirling, streaming, pouring and flowing. They like washing things outdoors, making bubbles, filling holes, watering seeds and watching birds splashing and preening in a bird bath. They love boats of wood, paper, bark or a leaf; wading, paddling, splashing around and swimming. Water is the life force of the planet; much of the world's climate is driven by the oceans and their currents.

Water sprite? Child?

Little child in little stream

Treasures in rock pool

In water we observe the marvellous metamorphosis of tadpoles to
frogs and toads and the emerging dragonfly. Water is thrilling when
rushing over a waterwheel (see instructions for making this, p. 88) or
waterfall, springing from a fountain, or moving in river or sea. Sometimes, after much rain, our kindergarten terrace drain could not cope.
But we enjoyed taking our chairs out to eat our snack in the 'ship' on the
4-inch high 'ocean'.

Water games

Painting: Paint a wall or paving with a bucket of water and a big brush.
Siphons, sieves, tubes, pieces of guttering and funnels all provide entertainment. Other activities are actually useful, especially in areas where water is
not so plentiful: filling a bucket or can from the water butt for watering
plants, or using washing-up water to wash the car.

Walnut boats: Blow half-shells filled with tiny gifts across a paddling pool.
Disguise and enhance the plastic by laying cloths of watery colours over it,
held down by stones, before filling.

Rafts: Peg corks together with cocktail sticks.

Ducks and Drakes: Take flattish pebbles, skim them low over the water and
see them hop.

Air (summer)

Feathers and bubbles are bewitching playthings. Children love to run after
snowflakes and falling leaves while they float away. Trees swaying, pipes
playing and clouds moving are all phenomena of airy movement. The
sylph or fairy is the elemental being of the air. Children like wings pinned
to their back, made simply of a long rectangle of coloured muslin attached
to the wrists. Dancing round the maypole, skipping, swinging, lying in a
hammock, throwing balls and running after hoops are joyful airy activities. Climbing a hedge, ladder or tree to the top enables the child to be
suspended for a moment above the earth. They love windmills, paper
streamers, kites, wind chimes and big flags. How better to find out what
air can do than to sail a boat, throw a paper plane or blow on the fire to
make it burn? A weather-vane turns in the moving air. Air brushes past the

Woven willow tree, or castle, kitchen, ship, nest, look-out

skin when children's hair flies, they lean on the wind, whoosh down the slide or ride on a seesaw. Balloons and windsocks are enduring toys. And everyone enjoys a picnic in the fresh air at the top of a hill.

Airy games

Throwing: Play with balls, hoops, frisbees, boomerangs and quoits.

Telephone: Remove one end of two tins, empty (and use) contents and wash well. Make a small hole in the centre of the bottom of each tin. Thread one long, thin piece of string through both holes, making a solid knot inside each tin. By pulling the string taut, two children can talk or listen into their microphone-cum-loudspeaker, up a tree, across a stream, out of the window . . . Try it with wire. From about 6 years.

Flying: Play with a tissue-paper butterfly or bird hanging from a twig.

Blowing: Blow feathers, tissue paper or sheep's wool balls about.

Fire or warmth (autumn)

Sunburn makes us only too aware of the sun's fiery power, but sunlight and warmth enable germination of seed, growth and ripening for harvest. We sometimes feel the fire of passion or inspiration, an inner experience of warmth and love. Children delight in butterflies and bees, creatures of the sun, and enjoy modelling with beeswax (see Appendix 2). A honeycomb is one of nature's marvels. Many homes today do not possess a chimney (tricky for Father Christmas), but smoke twirling out in mysterious shapes excites the imagination. An autumn bonfire fills the day with fine smells, and the night with strange colours and the elemental dancing salamanders or fire fairies; lanterns help show the way and a smoky baked potato fills the tummy.

Warmth games

Naturally many games warm one up through exertion, but warmth of heart and sociability is something they all have in common too.

Sand candles: Suspend a piece of wick tied to a horizontal stick over a hole made in sand or earth outdoors. Melt wax indoors slowly in a double saucepan ('water-bath'), i.e. always with water underneath, never without or it will boil and catch fire. Stay with it and have a fire blanket nearby, although in such a water-bath it should be safe. Use old stubs or new wax from a craft shop or beekeeper. Carry the melted wax (without the water-bath) carefully outdoors and fill the sandy or earthy space with the melted wax. When cooled, lift it out and admire the shape. Wash earth off but leave the sand. *Hot wax is very hot and sticks to you, but with the above precautions this is a wonderful activity.*

Candle dipping in winter or midsummer: Cover a table outdoors with old cloths or pretty paper. Decorate it with leafy twigs in summer; pine twigs, cones and rose hips are nice in winter. Prepare melted wax as above, then carry it outside and put it onto some kind of heater to keep it melted, such as you might use for camping or fondue, whilst still in the water-bath. Dress warmly in winter, with thinnish gloves. Everyone has a length of wick (from hardware or craft stores; they will tell you which one for which thickness of candle), say 20 cm long, and walks slowly round the table, dipping it into the wax as they go past. Do not leave the wick in the wax long or your growing candle will melt!

Candle decorating for outdoor birthdays or other celebrations: (1) Draw on white candles with wax crayons; (2) Make pictures or patterns with thin wax shapes warmed in the hand from coloured wax sheets to stick onto plain candles.

Beeswax modelling: This is a wonderful activity, also for warming the hands at any time of the year. Warm a piece by moving it in the palms; *keep it flat until soft*, then you can begin to model with it. When finished, flatten it again so it is easy to start next time. You can soften pieces which have become fat on a radiator or in a slow oven, but watch it or it may melt. Children under 6 need only a thin piece 5 × 5 cm or 5 cm diameter. Older ones can cope with larger pieces. Take care if wanting to have different colours together; do not *mix* them, just press them together so you can pull them apart. Do not roll it on a table or put it down anywhere while modelling or it will go hard again. Keep it in a clean place or it will pick up fluff. You can buy coloured or natural wax.

NOTE: *Mercurius or Myriad (See Crafts in Appendix 2) sell beautiful wax crayons, wax sheets and modelling beeswax.*

In summary

Playing games, working and celebrating together round the year, in tune with the changing seasons, offers repetitive security, and space and time for social and inner development. Such activities, contained largely within the seasonal round and the child's closer environment, give a wonderful sense of rhythm, protection and engagement with our immediate surroundings. Now, however, let us wander out of the garden into the wider world beyond.

7
Beyond the Garden Gate

Walking and hiking

'Up there it goes downhill.'

Your goal may be the top of a hill or mountain, yet often when you think you are almost there another top comes into view: a metaphor for life. The family may need encouragement (if they are not perpetually disappearing into the distance). Wise adults allow dawdling if there is no reason to hurry. This is quite healing for some children, especially the rather breathless or nervous ones. Leaving time to investigate decreases the need for chivvying. When you finally reach the top and the open view, you can be jubilant as you unpack the well-earned picnic.

Glowing cheeks, a good appetite and feeling of solidarity are rewards after long walks, where the speed of modern life slows to a child's pace. Adjust to the speed of the slowest, resting every hour or so. If children are used to walking, they can go long distances without complaining. On an eight-mile family trip, Nina, just 2, walked two miles and Sven, 4, all eight. We had many happy 'expeditions' in kindergarten. Three miles was not too far, once they were used to it. I saw two young parents glad to rest for their picnic after $1\frac{1}{2}$ hours' walk up 250 m height difference. But their 5-year-old didn't sit down *once*. Sandwich in hand, she was up the slope, down again, along a wall, over some steps, ready to be off again. A father of 3- and 5-year-olds nearby said, 'I'm *amazed* we made it! And we didn't even have to carry them!' Children love to revisit places and experiences. Naturally they also enjoy new things for wonder and surprise; you may all decide to change course on the way. Older children like to help plan the route, and especially enjoy going off with friends. Parents like to be invited to accompany a class on outings and see what they do, even taking days off for it. The UK government Early Years Framework states: '...where outdoor play space cannot be provided, outings should be planned and taken on a daily basis...'

In hilly places it is tempting to take short cuts, but as this can be eco-

Class hike with parents

logically damaging, one should stay on the paths. Picking up stones for cairns may alter the flow of water or otherwise cause erosion, so please wait until the top. There are splendid long distance walks such as coastal paths, Offa's Dyke in Wales, the South Downs Way in England, and other wonderful treks in your own locality, with places to stay or camp nearby. The Natural England organization (see Appendix 2) is planning a 2733-mile footpath round England and Wales. Each country has its own well-trodden paths. All hikes have particular attractions: historical, cultural, natural, archaeological. On coastal paths one finds caves and coves where smugglers operated with flashing lights, avoiding 'preventive men' (police). This makes exciting family reading, tucked up in a sleeping bag in a tent nearby under the stars. For children over 8 the story *Moonfleet* is wonderfully gripping (see Appendix 2). My children also loved *Three Men in a Boat*, by Jerome K. Jerome. There are shipwrecks to be seen, cliffs of screaming seabirds, swathes of flowers, wild hills or deep valleys with huge ferns. Tourist Offices offer maps and information. Your hike may include a ferry across a river or lake, on which you can usually take bikes too. Depending on the ages in your family or group, you may find the children manage more than the adults. Some spend a whole holiday walking. There are many wonderful national parks, and forest and nature reserves to refresh soul, body and spirit.

Most towns and cities have gardens, a river, pond or 'country park' just a walk or bus ride away. There the family can mark the seasons: have tea out, feed the ducks, see the male pheasant strutting in his fine spring coat or the moorhen with her chicks. There is plenty of time for children to travel and do more sophisticated things when teenagers or adults. Taking a walk in spring after a long winter can be so rewarding: finding small flowers and lambs, or seeing sunlight streaming through the ears of deer or rabbits. Sometimes you hear the wonderful sound of church bells ringing. Churchyards are peaceful places to rest in town or country.

Sucking a lemon or drinking fresh lemon or orange juice mixed with water quenches thirst. Sugary drinks and sweets create more thirst. Water is heavy but little sips go a long way so you may need less than you think. Dried fruit and nuts give quick nourishment. It is fun to have a cloth bag with dried fruit and nuts hanging down by your side as you go along (with family or class) for hands to find their way in (for nut allergy sufferers an additional bag with just fruit). The eyes in the back of your head sort out the greedy from the shy: lift the bag out in a particular direction. Cereal bars or biscuits, wrapped in rustly paper are a surprise. On a picnic, children enjoy finding a hidden place nearby to eat. Take a plastic box on walks for finds such as blackberries, wild plums and blueberries.

Action songs speak to children, helping swing the legs along. It is fun to invent them as you go along, sometimes based on a familiar one such as these lines. Children often have good suggestions to add.

Who'll help the sailor, sail along the boat? I will, I will, it's a joy to be afloat.
Who'll help the farmer, sowing out the wheat? I will, I will, with sturdy hands
*   and feet.*
Who'll help the garage man, underneath the car? I will, I will, clink, clank, tra, la.
Who'll help the milkman, going on his round? I will, I will, it only costs a pound.
Who'll help the fisherman, catching lots of fish? I will, I will, swish, swosh, swish.
Who'll help the children, feed the hungry chicks? I will, I will, peck, peck pick,
*   peck pick.*
Who'll help the rabbits, nibbling up their food? I will, I will, yum, it tastes so good.
Who'll help the happy birds, singing in the tree? I will, I will, tweet, tweet,
*   tweeeeeeeeeeeee.*
Who'll help Mandy, pegging out the clothes? I will, I will, shirts and hats and hose.
Who'll help Angus, sawing up the wood? I will, I will, whood, whoood, whooood.
Who'll help Grandma, knit beneath the tree? I will, I will, she's making socks,
*   you see.*
Who'll help Grandpa, reading in the shade? I will, I will, he's dropped his lemonade.

By the author, based on a song heard long ago

You may like to use the following tune, or another you know that will fit.

Singing songs or telling each other stories engages older ones. This chant suits any age. Someone says a phrase and everyone else repeats it (italics).

Flee, *Flee,*
Flee, fly, *Flee, fly,*
Flee, fly, flo, *Flee, fly, flo,*
Veesta, *Veesta.*
Kumalada, kumalada, kumalada, veesta,
Kumalada, kumalada, kumalada, veesta.
Oh, no, no, no-no, da veesta.
Oh, no, no, no-no, da veesta.
Ee ne mee ne, des amee ne, oo-aah, oo-aahla mee ne, Ee ne mee ne, des amee ne, oo-aah, oo-aah.
Ee ne mee ne, des amee ne, oo-aah, oo-aahla meene, Ee ne mee ne, des amee ne, oo-aah, oo-aah.
Atcha katcha koomaratcha, oo-aah, oo-aah
Atcha katcha koomaratcha, oo-aah, oo-aah
Bee, Billy, oaten, doten, doh, doh, skideeten, dutten, Shhhhhhhhhhhhhhhhhhhhhhhhhhhhhhhhh.
Bee, Billy, oaten, doten, doh, doh, skideeten, dutten, Shhhhhhhhhhhhhhhhhhhhhhhhhhhhhhhhhhh.

Source unknown

It is pleasant to wander along in silence, buried in one's own thoughts. It is common nowadays to see not only adults but children walking, jogging, and cycling using a mobile phone or iPod, so that they cannot hear nature's songs!

After a long, wet walk, it is cosy to have a warm drink, draw the curtains and cuddle up in a blanket. Even if only for half an hour, this allows the body a little recuperation.

Carrying belongings

Children like to feel independent with their own rucksack. However, some parents carry their own large one plus their children's, but encouraging words

Rucksack, good shoes, stick and twig,
essential hiking equipment

help: 'I'm so pleased you are big enough to carry your own bag/doll/coat now.'

At 3 and 4, even 2, children happily pack up and carry their own rucksacks. Of course little ones just have dolly, cup, hanky and bun, but older children can carry more. Young ones love taking a doll's pushchair for a short walk.

What if children with bikes, scooters or toy prams don't want to ride or push them all the way? Are they old and strong enough actually to do so, or is it all right for us to carry them when they are tired of it? You may need to decide for them before you set out. Some children are very determined and will carry on to dropping point, while others seek a convenient 'shelf' in the adult. Children may like to help carry the shopping to the car, bus or even home—good exercise. An unused pushchair for light or heavier items makes an excellent shopping basket which children are eager to push. When bikes, trikes and various wheeled toys get too fast, one can report a speed limit of 374 mph, so they need to apply their brakes and change gear. The movement on such equipment is almost solely in the legs, so I believe it is wise to limit this one-sided activity.

Children like a knapsack or bag for collecting treasures. My husband and I took two children of 5 and 8, unused to walking, for an autumn hike in the dunes. Our map, or our intelligence, didn't tally with the paths. We walked much further than planned, eventually coming to the promised pancake restaurant. Both children had a rucksack, gradually filling it with special finds: leaves of every hue, cones, wood. That helped keep them going, besides holding a hand or sharing a big brave hug, especially the younger one when he said we had to carry him (which we couldn't). We were all happy with our achievement.

I had a small 'magic bag' for the family and kindergarten in which I kept everything we might need. It contained soap leaves, a flannel, string, plasters, penknife, small cut-all scissors, elastic, rubber bands, safety pins, needle, buttons and thread, paper and pencil, sellotape and glue. It came in useful many times. With the string we once tied up the pushchair axle; another time we came to the rescue of someone whose suitcase broke at the station, spilling its contents onto the floor.

Safety tips

Thunderstorms: Try to seek shelter in a building or car. Keep away from the windows and doors. Otherwise avoid lakes, rivers and tall objects: trees, towers, telegraph poles, etc. Go downhill if you are on a ridge or peak. Crouch down low, so you are not a protruding object, with your feet together. Do not lie down as lightning can move along the ground. Lightning usually strikes into the most prominent point. If you are in a forest, go to the middle of a clearing if possible.

Sun: Put sun lotion, hats and shirts on your children; give them water.

Water and weather: Being swept out to sea when swimming or in dinghies is avoidable by checking the weather and local situation. Squalls can come up quickly, also on lakes.

Waterfalls: Do not play beneath these as stones may fall with the water.

Throwing: Never allow children to throw anything downhill or off a cliff. There may be someone below.

Bicycles

I prefer simple bikes for younger children despite the strong prestige element; they grow out of them so quickly. It is helpful for parents to share thoughts with friends. Do they actually need 27 gears, or are five enough? It is a pleasure to see children out riding with friends, family or even grandparents.

This way, that way . . .

There are incredible contraptions, new, second-hand or for rent: tandems with two or three children on the back, trailers and recumbents ('stretch'-bikes) for families and what-have-you. Disabled children can ride tricycles, four-wheeled recumbents or be in trailers. Child seats that clip on in front of the adult are cosy, like a penguin chick. You can buy 'Slime', from bike shops to squirt into punctured tyres; it closes the hole (unless really big) and enables you to get home, sealing the following punctures immediately too.

Cycle routes are best separated from horses, which render the ground uncyclable or almost unwalkable. Many people are within a few miles of a dedicated route. Some cycleways in the UK are set aside for mountain bikes so children can get out and have their fun and skilful practice; more would be better. Many mountain bikers in fact do not want to do tricks, but merely cycle in wilder areas. In some countries (but not the UK!) it is common for cyclists to have priority on many roads (and even some roundabouts in Holland).

It is fun to cycle along a towpath, camping at night. The boats overtake on the straight but you do at the locks. My children dubbed country roads with grass pushing through the tarmac in the centre 'motorways'. In Mediterranean climates, oleanders, forsythia and geraniums grow by roads, and cushions of sage and thyme push into the edges—beautiful to ride or walk along. Dandelions, soapwort and other plants growing locally by the wayside are so pretty too.

Public access and transport

Buses and trains are splendid methods of transport for children. Not cooped up as in cars, they can chat to their companions better, see out of big windows and move more freely.

A grandmother spoke of the regular days she looked after her 2- and 3-year-old grandchildren. Not being keen on car travel, they always went by 47 bus and then train to their uncle. Once when it was nearly time to alight she said they had to get off now, whereupon the youngest waggled her finger at her grandmother and said, 'Not until it stops.'

What about walking children to school? In the 'walking bus', children wearing fluorescent clothing walk in pairs with a leader and guard to and from school to a proper timetable, picking up others at particular 'bus

School run—riding on the back or running alongside

School run

stops' on the way. The 'cycle train' works in a similar way, but the riders cycle behind each other with an adult in front and behind. If you *have* to drive to and from school, you could leave the car a little way away and walk the rest, thereby helping congestion at school gates. An infant school in London has a government-backed scheme for children on foot-scooters, for which they have to take proficiency tests.

The UK Countryside and Rights of Way Act allows access to much mountain, moor, down, heath and forest. Naturally the same courtesy and respect for animals, the land and its owners applies as anywhere. New Ordnance Survey maps show accessible land in pale yellow with an orange border. Many long distance hikes, open gardens and nature reserves are accessible by public transport here and in Europe, and they generally have special rates for families including single parents; rail and bus services offer special deals. One hopes for public transport costs to go down, encouraging more people to use it.

A 17-year-old sank into her bus seat. 'I can't believe it's £4.80 just to Crawley! That's half my money gone already.'

Some areas really do help the environment through their exemplary timetables, routes and fares. In London, school children travel free on buses. Most longer-distance UK trains have a 'quiet carriage' away from mobiles and iPods, which is a good place for children (until they have their own . . .). I am not aware of a scheme giving free train and bus passes to poorer families, but this would be an important incentive to venture out of doors. A special treat for my children was to walk to the nearby small station to watch the trains with Grandpa. Large stations can be very noisy, but older children enjoy train-spotting anywhere. It is also fun to count the number of goods trucks going by.

19 Seven nations at outdoor carnival

20 Hoku Lani and her Hawaiian lei

21 Flowers for Whitsun

22 Maypole

23 Midsummer festival game

24 Outdoors brought indoors, Harvest and Michaelmas

25 Autumn mobile with grains, seeds and felt mice

26 Pinecone 'hedgehog'

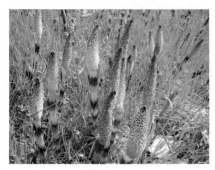

27 Horsetail (equisetum) 'gnomes'
  before opening

28 Horsetail opening

29 Happy hike

30 The author hiking with her (then) young family

31 Sven and friends' sleeping arrangements

Orientation

It is fun to orientate yourself with natural compasses.

1. Locate the sun halfway between the hour hand of your watch and the 12; 12 points approximately south.
2. Hang a long magnet from a thread, or
3. Put a magnet onto a cork slice floating on water; it will turn north-south (for 2. and 3. you need to see some sunshine to tell which is north and which south!).
4. Trees show north by their mossy side; the sun dries out the south-facing one.
5. Trees incline away from prevailing winds (in much of Britain from the south-west).
6. Or use a proper compass! A Global Positioning System is interesting yet unchallenging.

Other hints: currents of tidal rivers pull anchored boats with them, so they point towards the flow and you know if the tide is going in or out. Some tidal rivers are dangerous, so ask locally. A lady from mainland Europe wanted to go to England, as she heard that the rivers there ran backwards as well as forwards (i.e. the tide coming *in* as well as the usual *out*flow).

Sometimes it's fun to get lost *on purpose*. Take turns to choose which way at each crossing or junction, sniffing the air and following your nose. Or you can just go right, left, right, left. This can cause hilarity as you may end up where you started but that is all part of the fun. It may mean you have to go somewhere you *really* don't want to, but you have to stick to the rules or agree beforehand to change them, with a forfeit, e.g. a goodie less. Play this on foot, by bicycle or in the car; we found the most fun was on our bikes in a place we did not know. We might watch the sun for a sense of direction but did not really want a clue. Amazement could follow when looking at the map at half-time (time allowed to get home again). Alternatively, take the first bus (to anywhere) that leaves from your nearest bus station, or ask at the train station for tickets costing a certain amount and see where they take you.

Picnics

You may find pieces of bark for plates, or wood that lends itself to carving into a knife or spoon. I believe children, especially boys, need to have a

Picnic tables and stools at Standen, National Trust

penknife when they are old enough to handle it safely, maybe from about 6. Children from 2 or 3 can use a small knife in the kitchen under supervision. Like so many other potentially dangerous things, they can respect and use them properly only if they have the chance to learn. It is a challenge to some adults to find the trust to allow it. Forbidden things, like swear words and matches, are also attractive. 'We will light the fire/ candle together, and when you are bigger you can do it on your own' may satisfy the child. A 2- or 3-year-old can light a candle or fire under supervision, and alone from about 7 if deemed responsible, with an adult in the vicinity. Swear words can be ignored, particularly in young children as they are generally only copying, or one can ignore the child if he or she wants something with it. Or say, 'I would rather hear grown-up language,' or, 'I couldn't really hear what you said,' in an innocent voice, or be inspired in the moment, but getting cross or making a fuss does not help. Often one cannot find out where it was learnt.

Children enjoy making a picnic, on their own or with guidance. I prefer refillable bottles and food in reusable boxes to pre-packaged goods (healthier, and these also help avoid landfill and resources problems). Baskets are attractive for carrying everything. If hot without shade, keep

Kindergarten children sawing wood for the fire

drinks and meltable items in a hole, best in water. The meal is attractive with napkins, flowers and leaves on the picnic cloth or garden table. Pop a thin cloth into the picnic basket. Fallen autumn leaves can provide a cloth. Children love to sweep a messy place clean with twigs, then decorate with twigs, stones or flowers before arranging the food. In the dark, put a candle in an apple in the centre of each plate. An elderly friend said saying grace helps the digestion. It is nice to speak a simple one before picnics too, then join hands and say: 'May the meal be blessed, and peace be on the earth.' One can end holding hands, saying, 'Thank you for our meal.' Eating outdoors may encourage running around, yet if children are used to structure and rhythm, it should be easy to keep everyone together. You can say anyone who leaves their place does not get any more to eat. Giving not more than one or two things at a time helps too. This needs to start at home from a very early age, not allowing getting up and down from the table for instance, having meals at the same times every day, sitting at the meal with an adult always present as a model and so on. I have written about this in my book *Well, I Wonder*.

> *Bread is a lovely thing to eat,*
> *God bless the barley and the wheat.*
> *A lovely thing to breathe is air,*

God bless the sunshine everywhere.
The world is a lovely place to know,
God bless the folks that come and go.
Alive is a lovely thing to be,
Giver of life, we say: bless Thee!

H.M. Sarson

Everyone can share in carrying the picnic. In kindergarten, we needed thermoses of herb tea, cups, teaspoons and a container of müesli, sandwiches, etc. To save luggage we ate our food from the cups after a drink. Sometimes we carried hoops, ropes or balls. Old cut-up (camping) sleeping mats provided insulation for sitting. Hygiene on a picnic is not very easy, especially if on foot. You can wash hands before leaving home and take water, soap and a spade. Otherwise nature will keep you clean, I think; the more time children spend under the sky, the stronger their immune system will be. Sometimes you may be near water anyway. A small bottle suffices for washing cuts and scrapes. I recommend always washing hands on return.

Campfire

12 November: Baked potatoes and chestnuts at fire site under 'weather'. Hope to do it again next week, maybe under *other* weather. The children said it only started to pour *after* we'd finished eating so it would put the fire out and we wouldn't need to. Children are so imaginatively positive. When the heavens opened completely, we sheltered under nearby bushes for the story, enjoying just a fine spray in our cosy 'house'. My silent thanks went to the parents for making these moments possible by kitting the children out properly, and for their support and trust.

19 November: Plant bulbs near fire site.

25 February: Saw bulbs coming up. Exciting!

Gathering fallen wood for the fire, struggling with a heavy cart and carrying the equipment kept the children warm. We sat round the fire on planks and logs we had gradually carried there ourselves. On cold days, a cup of soup or herb tea (our own) in one hand and half a hot potato with mild yeast extract and organic margarine in the other was a happy event.

Sean, 5, had never liked potatoes. Yet the sight of everyone enjoying theirs wetted his lips and he tried a tiny bit. Next time he had a bit more, then more still, until he was glad of the spare bit. Cheeks glowed, social life blossomed in squeezing up for others, sharing food and conversation. Our word 'hearth' is close to 'heart'. I was blessed with assistants who supported me and didn't mind getting a bit grubby and fire-smelly.

16 February: The children sat still after break, quietly looking at the fire, with hardly a word.

An old saucepan with string or wire tied round the rim and three lengths tied from it upwards to attach to a tripod of sticks for porridge or soup makes a fantastic cauldron.

In and over the outdoor fire you can roast apples, sausages, cheese, potatoes, marshmallows and bread dough. For garlic bread, halve a baguette lengthways, put butter, chopped or squeezed garlic, salt, lemon juice and herbs inside, then toast it on a grille or held skewered onto two sticks. Bake a thin piece of uncooked dough by wrapping it round a longish stick and holding it over the fire. It rises and bakes quite quickly. Take care that the stick does not contain toxic material, e.g. laurel. Children like to whittle their stick. I believe they need to be close enough to the fire to feed it and feel the heat (under an adult's eagle but imperceptible eye), on the side away from the smoke.

A consultant was to give a talk to parents and practitioners about his design for their school. 'But just don't mention fire!' said the head teacher. I remain convinced that if children are allowed to have an open fire, learn how to deal with it in a controlled, sensible way and understand the risks, they are likely to respect it. Many outdoor fires are caused by those without such experience. Accidents are usually the result of some careless activity such as waving burning sticks around, putting fireworks in the fire, running near or jumping over it. Synthetic material may melt and stick to the skin. Ask your local wildlife trust whether they are running a course on fire-lighting skills and fire safety. Fire Stations also give advice.

It is good to build a brick or stone fireplace. Alternatively, there are portable BBQs—just a 40 cm wide metal dish with wire stand and grid. They can be cleaned and reused. You need to be certain you can keep the fire under control: do not make one in dry weather or near dry undergrowth, or too big for your circumstances, or in a wind. Water or a fire beater must be nearby. Only make a fire in a designated fire site and ensure it is out properly when you leave. Adults know who may be trusted to light matches and dispose of them safely. Younger children may be given a taper, lit from a match that one has lit oneself. It is good to remember and use children's natural imitation up to about the age of 8: give the taper in a respectful, careful way, holding it with one hand while guarding the flame by cupping the other hand behind it. This guarding hand gives a feeling of restraint. Playing about means it is not allowed next time, a challenge to learn it properly. One has to be careful what is burnt. Could it be recycled? Does it contain toxins (e.g. chemical preservatives)?

If you light a bonfire in autumn, look inside first for hibernating hedge-hogs. Move them with leather gloves to a similar place, e.g. pile of sticks or leaves. Or make another fire elsewhere. It is best to build the fire just before lighting because of this. Children may like to feed the roses with the potassium-rich ashes from the fire.

Cooking skills are sorely lacking today; campfires can create an early interest.

Recipes

Burgers: 500 grams mince or meat substitute, 1 egg, 1 onion, breadcrumbs, seasoning. Roll into shapes.

Kebabs: Children find sticks to spear vegetables and fruits.

Potatoes: Rub fat over skin, prick and put in fire. Remove before burnt, brush ash off.

Pudding: Cut unpeeled bananas lengthways, put chocolate inside, wrap in foil and bake. (Wash and re-use foil.)

Specials

Patio heater: Put on another jumper and socks instead.

Pencil: The (cold) charcoaly end of a burnt stick.

Sausage: You know if this is cooked when you can write with it!

Camping

We endeavoured to keep our luggage as modest as possible (also for easier riding on bikes). You can decant things into small pots and boxes, and do without a lot of things. This is excellent discipline and goes for walking holidays too! I hope the reader will be inspired to leave physical baggage behind and discover how much soul baggage will fall away with it under the sky. What do we *really, actually* need?

Children like staying on a farm or beach, hiking in the hills or camping. If camping very simply, you can have everything down to a fine art on arrival—everything unloaded, tent up, supper cooking within 20 minutes. Our youngest was 9 on our first biking holiday (when I was a lone parent) but one could start younger. She carried the dome tent on her bike rack (for three people, into which we fitted five, so there was less to carry). When the children were older we had the luxury of another small tent! I carried the stove with fitting saucepans in my front basket, and the three boys and I had panniers for the rest. A total of two small towels were enough for all together, one for washing and one for swimming. Whoever got there first was the lucky one as it was probably still dry. In France someone called them our *mouchoirs* (handkerchiefs).

Two smallish plastic bowls double for salad, mixing food and washing up. One large and one small cooking knife are enough; cereal bowls can be plates or cups. With a storm-kettle you can safely boil up the tea or soup, using whatever combustible material is around: twigs, dry grass... String is indispensable, for hanging up washing, tying up a mudguard, etc. Small clothes pegs are useful, yet you can also push the ends of your washing through doubled, twisted string and hang it up like that. A small plastic tarpaulin is handy as a windbreak or roof, tied on to something with your string. You can shelter under it, huddled together on a rainy walk. A wooden mallet or log is useful for banging pegs into hard ground. Of course caravans, camper vans and big tents are fine, yet a small tent brings bigger challenges and perhaps even more fun.

One can become quite resourceful, especially avoiding sophisticated campsites which are noisy and have everything. It is magical to sleep under the stars without shelter, and awe-inspiring to spend a stormy, wet night progressively tightening and loosening the guy ropes to stop your little tent blowing away. Some of the time it may be nearly blown flat, but when you see big tents blown to bits you will be glad you decided to leave most of your home behind.

A friend told her young daughter about their proposed camping trip with special beds and stove for cooking. Emma said, 'What for? Why not just stay at home?'

Swimming and boating

Swimming is wonderful also for disabled children; they can use buoyancy aids and feel a freedom with their limbs not possible on land. I once worked in a school for disabled children where the favourite pursuit was the small outdoor pool.

A calmish sea, being buoyant, makes learning to swim easier. Unpolluted rivers are generally safe for teaching children to swim. You can find out about possible currents, dangerous weirs and unexpected depths.

A holiday near water is a joy for children. There may be rock pools or tide-formed lagoons to explore. Sandy cliffs, usually full of nesting birds, are often eroding, so children may not necessarily dig into or run up and down them, but rocky cliffs invite scrambling. Some children join climbing clubs to scale the heights with ropes, such as on the Welsh Gower Peninsular.

The author taking a break from paddling with her husband

Paddling their home-made raft

Paddling their double-sized home-made raft

Quiet fishing is not only for Dads

Drawbridge

> Watching wildlife near water is a particular pleasure, such as wading birds poking about for worms or ducks up-tailing. The osprey makes a well in the water as it swoops in to catch its dinner in its claws. As the water closes up again it rushes into a peak, pushing the heavy, flapping bird with fish upwards, enabling it to take off again. It shakes itself to remove the water, then turns its dinner forwards as it flies on, making it aerodynamic.

A narrowboat canal trip is a treat, not least when operating locks and going over aqueducts. Any kind of boat is marvellous for children, especially with unruffled but watchful adults around.

Activities for older children and young people

'I can't get up this slope, it's too steep and slippery.' 'Try round here under this bush, you can hang onto the branch and heave yourself up.' 'Oh, cool!' Two guides helped each other in their challenging situation. Some teenagers find scouts, girl guides and girl scouts 'uncool', yet once smitten they become very enthusiastic. Children can join Beavers from 6 years old, then Cubs and Brownies before Scouts and Guides. Scouting and other youth camps provide varied skills practice for young people, even survival techniques. Peer power is strong: young people join when given incentives for exciting and fulfilling activities, thereby drawing them away from other, less constructive ones. The international 100-year Scouting Jamboree of 2007 drew together hundreds of thousands of young people from all over the world.

Vandalism occurs even in rural areas. Policing only partially solves the problem, whereas offering constructive and exciting things that seem 'cool' is very effective. There are many excellent schemes within cities as well as the country. (See 'Education', 'Environment' and 'Playground ... Creation' in Appendix 2).

In summary

Adventuring gradually into the wider world ensures a gradual broadening of human experience. Let us help our children to grow in wisdom and courage by increasingly offering them voyages beyond the garden gate. In the following chapter, by contrast, we come back closer to home to explore how children can transform their natural environment and so engage actively and positively with it.

8

CHILD AND WILDLIFE FRIENDLY GARDENING*

Plants for children

'When are you going to start again?' asked Glen and Abbie, peering over the fence and eagerly clutching their rakes. The 6- and 4-year-olds had been helping me garden all that week and were anxiously waiting to begin again.

Children can observe the wonder of nature in an old rose stem; bent and tied down, it sprouts to produce beautiful blossoms. Fallen trees may sprout into the vertical, creating a child's playground. Plants force themselves out of asphalt towards light and warmth. This incredible life-force can be seen in a cut-off leek or half-cabbage: they continue to grow; so do parsnips and carrots planted back in the earth, or with their tops left in a saucer of water.

'You have a good garden but the roses must be fenced off,' inspectors told a child-minder. How were the children to smell and touch them? Once pricked, they are careful. Wild-flower meadows and moss are a treat for insects; mown paths through meadows are a treat for children. Children enjoy seeing how some plants close their petals at sundown, like the daisy, while others follow the path of the sun, such as the sunflower. 'Jack-goes-to-bed-at-noon' really closes its petals at midday. You can observe evening primrose flowers actually opening at dusk.

Poisonous plants in Britain are listed in Appendix 2. Other countries have their own. Please do not take plants from the wild; buy from a nursery. Take care with non-native, invasive plants (beware nurseries selling them). Bamboo is satisfying for play, but is very invasive. A local horticulturalist will advise you. Using plants best suited to your garden's conditions is a sustainable method of cultivation.

---

* See also 'Gardening with Young Children' in Appendix 2.

The plants mentioned here are not a comprehensive list, just some suggestions...

Plant characteristics

Some plants flower with sweet fragrances in winter. Fruit blossom flying off the trees is a joyful sight. Summer brings a flood of flowers: heavenly colours clamber over fences in single petals or like a ballet tutu with textures from prickles and sturdy leaves to translucent petals. Children shower fallen petals over the birthday table. Autumn fills the world with glory.

There is beauty in cut wood, like the pink fresh yew or patterned walnut. Trees grow into myriad shapes; many carry on growing when hollow. Magnificent oaks have gnarled and knobbled trunks; yew wraps its roots around rocks and makes extraordinary trunk forms.

Planting for scent: azalea, carnation, chimonanthus (winter sweet), freesia, all herbs, honeysuckle (including the winter *Lonicera fragrans*), lilac, lime tree in flower, philadelphus (mock orange), varieties of pinks (dianthus), rose, stock, sweet pea, sweet william, viburnum, violet, wallflower.

Planting for shapes: aquilegia, berberis (barberry), bluebell, primula (candelabra varieties), campanula (Canterbury bells), chrysanthemum, cistus (petals delicate as a butterfly wing), clematis varieties (including the wild old man's beard), cornflower, cosmos, creeping Jenny, cyclamen, daffodil, davidia ('handkerchief' or 'dove' tree), delphinium, fig leaves and its fruit (actually an inside-out flower), forget-me-not, foxglove, geranium (cranesbill), *Gingko biloba* ('butterfly' leaves), golden rod, hollyhock, iris (including the wetland yellow flag), Japanese quince, *Kalmia latifolia*, ladies' mantle, London pride, mesembryanthemum, Michaelmas daisy, morning glory, nasturtium, pansy, passion flower, pea, pelargonium varieties, peony, penstemon (flowers until December), periwinkle, phlox, red hot poker, sedum varieties, snapdragon, snowdrop, sunflowers, thrift (sea pink on its little green cushion), umbrella plants (e.g. dill, fennel and lovage), water lilies.

Planting for autumn colour: amelanchia, beech, berberis (barberry), birch, cherry, crab apples, forsythia, maples, vine, Virginia creeper.

Planting for or trailing over railings, a trellis or pergola: clematis, honey-suckle, hops, jasmine, morning glory, passion flower, roses, runner beans, vine, Virginia creeper, wisteria.

Providing seeds and berries

A bush dripping with berries is a heart-warming joy for birds' tummies and our eyes. Various plants are difficult to protect, so you may decide to give in gracefully and share with the birds. All fruits attract birds so some may need netting.

Trees, climbers and shrubs: alder, amelanchier, arbutus (strawberry tree), ash, berberis (barberry), beech, blackberry, blackthorn (sloe), buckthorn, cedar, Chilean myrtle, clematis, cotoneaster, dogwood, elder, field maple, gorse, guelder rose, hawthorn, hazel, holly, hornbeam, ivy, juniper, larch, lime tree, loganberry, lupin, mahonia, mulberry, passion flower, poppy, pyracantha (firethorn), roses (especially old and wild varieties), rowan, sandthorn, Scots pine, silver birch, snowberry, spruce.

Annuals and perennials: alkanet, astilbe, borage, calendula, candytuft, chrysanthemum, comfrey, dill, elder, evening primrose, fennel, foxglove, flax, hollyhock, honesty, scabious, lavender, lemon balm, lovage, love-in-a-mist, mallow, marjoram, marsh marigold, Michaelmas daisy, nasturtium, nettles, oregano, pink, poppy, *Sedum spectabile*, snapdragon, spirea, sunflower, sweet pea, thistles, thyme, valerian, wallflower, water mint, many weeds, wild strawberry and raspberry, willowherb.

Providing pollen and nectar

Plants of early spring★ provide much needed food on a warm day when insects venture out; most flower before the leaves open, bringing hope after the winter. Children love to see the first bees after the winter, then the first butterfly and ladybird.

Trees, climbers and shrubs: berberis (barberry), brambles (blackberry), buddleia (butterflies), camellia★ (looks like roses in winter), *Clematis montana*,★ cornus (dogwood) varieties,★ dianthus varieties, forsythia,★ all fruit trees, heathers,★ *Hamamelis mollis* (witchhazel),★ hebe varieties, horse chestnut, *Hydrangea petiolaris* (clings to walls), chaenomeles (flowering quince),★ lilac, magnolia,★ oak, passion flower, potentilla, roses, sunflower, sweet chestnut, viburnum varieties,★ winter honeysuckle,★ winter jasmine,★ wintersweet (*Chimonanthus praecox*),★ wisteria.

Annuals and perennials: astilbe, beans, black-eyed Susan, borage, buddleia, cabbage, chamomile, Christmas rose,★ crocus,★ eschscholtzia (Californian poppy), fuchsia, gypsophila, honesty, honeysuckle (including the winter one,★ hops, hypericum, *Iris reticulata*,★ mints, morning glory, nettle, paeony, pasque flower, peas, primrose,★ rosemary, sweet pea, thistle, thyme, valerian, various fruits and vegetables.

Plants for tea infusions

Birch (leaves), fennel (seeds), lemon balm, lemon verbena, lime (blossom), mint, raspberry, rose (hips), sweet cicely, and many other herbs.

Tall plants for hiding and disappearing

Fennel (herb), Jerusalem and globe artichokes, lovage, runner beans, sprouting broccoli and rosemary amongst other tall herbs, flowers and vegetables. If paths are winding rather than straight, then a secret garden appears.

Plants for topiary

Bay, box and yew lend themselves to cutting into shapes. We really liked my father's animals along a hedge, but one little bush cut into something is special too.

The kitchen (fruit, herb and vegetable) garden

It is wonderful for children to grow fruit and vegetables: healthy and fresh without 'food miles'. They enjoy growing things for their lunch boxes. Vegetables and fruit have pretty flowers that do not last long as they are busy turning themselves into food, so mixing other flowers between them is attractive, especially 'companion plants' (see p. 175).

'I shouldn't think there's much goodness in that,' someone said to me one January as I picked weeds with the children for salad. Her family ate hothouse lettuce from abroad. There are many vitamins and minerals in freshly gathered weeds. Use leaves of daisies, dandelions, chickweed, plantain, millefoil, chicory, sorrel, nettles, winter cress, miner's lettuce and others. Pick them away from roads and chemically treated fields. Serve with cold-pressed sunflower, rapeseed or olive oil, lemon juice, herbs and a boiled egg, cream or yoghurt (all organic if possible). You can lightly cook many wild plants as a vegetable, for example Alexanders (poor man's asparagus), chickweed (poor man's spinach), nettle, comfrey and fat hen.

Vegetables and salads

Beans, broccoli, cabbage, carrots, cauliflower, chard, garlic, gourds (including courgettes), leeks, lettuce, onions, parsnips, peas, potatoes, pumpkins (including fancy varieties), tomatoes, wood sorrel (add a little to salads and soups). Many of these do not need deep soil; an old sink or bowl with drainage does well. Water in the morning, as slugs like the damp and eat at night.

If you grow many vegetables, it is helpful to rotate your order of crops annually to help keep the soil fertile and ward off disease. The main thing is not to have the same family in the same place the following year. The following is a suggestion for rotation.

1. Legumes (peas, beans, clover for green manure)
2. Roots (carrots, parsnips, turnips)
3. Solanaceous (tomatoes, potatoes, peppers)
4. Brassicas (cabbage, sprouts, broccoli, radish)
5. Alliums (onions, shallots, garlic)
6. Cucurbits (courgettes, squash, cucumber)

Salads and spinach can be grown anywhere in between.

Fruit (some are mentioned under berries above)

Apple, blackthorn (sloe), cherry, crab apple, currants, fig, gooseberries, grape vine, pear, plum, quince, rose (hip), wild and garden strawberries and raspberries. Fruit trees can be trained against a wall or fence, taking up little space.

Herbs

These pretty plants add scents to the garden. Cats love to lie on catmint. Many herbs are a magnet for bees. Allow part of herb plants to flower for insect food, but keep some cut so it continues growing. Cut fresh to add to salads and cooking, and make tea infusions with fresh and dried herbs. They enhance a vase of flowers too. Chives, dill, fennel and parsley are easy to sow and grow. Once established, most herbs will sprout every year. They look beautiful spilling over paths, steps, walls or paving.

> *Summer Pudding*: for children to make with fruit they grew and/or gathered. Briefly simmer 500 grams soft fruit; cut 8 slices white bread with crusts, to line a pudding basin. Fill with the fruit, put bread slices on top. Place small plate on top, weigh down with something heavy. Leave overnight for juice to soak through, turn onto dish.

Planting

Many spring flowers like a dappled, shady area, whereas vegetables need the sunniest, most fertile area. A wild–flower meadow needs the poorest, unfed soil, which makes it desperate to go to seed and therefore flowers first. Spring bulbs may be planted (in autumn) anywhere.

You can take the following into account to guide you in your choice: annual movement and height of sun round the garden; areas hot and dry in summer yet without sun and remaining wet in winter; frost pockets; places remaining damp and cool; windy corners; sandy, clay, loamy, alkaline or acid soil. Your nursery, or gardening books (see Appendix 2) will advise you which plants like to go where.

> *A little brown bulb went to sleep underground;*
> *In his little brown nightie he slept very sound.*
> *Old Winter, he roared and he raged overhead,*
> *But the bulb didn't even turn over in bed.*
> *When Spring came dancing over the lea,*
> *With finger on lip, just as soft as can be,*
> *The little brown bulb, he lifted his head,*
> *Split up his nightie and JUMPED out of bed!*

Author unknown

Children like to hide under a big cloth for this verse, jumping up at the end.

For tree planting:

I had a little nut tree, nothing would it bear
But a silver nutmeg and a golden pear;
The King of Spain's daughter came to visit me,
All for the sake of my little nut tree.
I skipped over water, I danced over sea,
And all the birds in the air couldn't catch me.

Old rhyme

Young children enjoy sharing your garden bed (and climbing into the other one!). Older children like to have their own patch. Giving them a pretty one where some plants are already growing is an excellent beginning. Give children seeds of different shapes and sizes. Mix tiny ones with sand for thinner sowing. Toilet rolls make good mini-pots for sowing; plant later complete (the cardboard becomes compost). Roses, jasmine or passion flowers can cover a drainpipe or wall or grow in tubs. Tubs need regular watering in dry weather. Take care children do not drown the plants in their enthusiasm! They can form a responsible habit of checking every day and watering if necessary. Gardens can withstand long, dry spells with plenty of humus and mulch. They send roots down to find water and so are safe; if receiving only a little water or rain, roots rush to the

Ryan gardening

Extra water-saving

surface and die of thirst. One advantage of growing organically or bio-dynamically is that you do not have to worry about the children ingesting any toxic fertilizer, pesticide or herbicide. Experts say the soil and therefore the plants are stronger and healthier, which has a beneficial effect on human health.

Children's hands will become grubby when outdoors. Rinsing them in a bucket of water first avoids dirtying the soap. (Use gardener's soap for very dirty or oily hands.)

Beds

Flower, fruit and vegetable beds for children are best if easily accessible from both sides and not too far away from house or classroom. Winding paths or stepping stones of old bricks, paving or roof tiles are attractive. Beds can have interesting shapes. A border of paving or lawn helps keep it all together. Some shrubs and herbs lend themselves to spilling over the edge of the bed.

Raised beds

These are raised above ground level. They never get compacted through trampling and need no digging. Holding moisture, warmth and light, they aid growth. With enough humus, they work equally well in heavy soil by helping drainage, or in sandy soil by preventing water from draining away too fast. Many are hillocks or heaped up earth a few inches high: long, round, spiral or any shape. Plants can grow on top and all around. If built within walls of beams, boards or brick, they are excellent for children in wheelchairs. Rectangular units of wood or recycled plastic are available in various sizes. Or make them yourself from long logs, old bricks or planks and boards with posts and pegs. They can stand on concrete or tarmac if necessary, with rubble at the bottom, drainage holes and good soil. Slugs and snails may hide in the edging. Half barrels and old tyres make small raised beds, pretty when plants spill over the edges. Beans or sweet peas growing up bamboo poles in them look lovely.

Raised bed

Raised bed for children in wheelchairs

Harvesting

A great joy is gathering what you have grown, then eating it or putting it in a vase. 'Mum, not marrow and beans *again!*' said my children when there was a glut and all our friends had been supplied. You can freeze, bottle or dry your harvest of course. Jam, juice, syrup and chutney are all excellent to preserve with children. Bunches of herbs, apple rings and strings of onions and garlic are easy to do. Rubbing dried herbs between the hands to put in a jar smells wonderful. Blackberries are an example of what people without a garden can gather. Seeing the whole process through from start to finish is wholesome and of particular educational value.

Weeds

Weeds tell you about the quality of your soil and are often beautiful plants which you prefer to have elsewhere. They are best removed before going to seed. If they do set seed, keep them separate from the compost heap. Patches of nettles, brambles and thistles are good for caterpillars, butterflies and risks! Nettles and comfrey add rich nutrients to compost.

Garden book

It is useful to keep a garden diary, containing for instance the names of plants, reminders about what is to be done, wildlife observed, pond details and what has not worked. Children like to draw or cut out colourful pictures of what has been planted and stick them in, write stories and see what there is to do. It can include a garden plan with plant names and future ideas.

This is a sample of part of a month from the 'what-to-do section' in my home garden book:

MAY: Prune forsythia. Trim camellia. Sow beans round bamboo wigwam. Lie under apple tree. Say hello to frogs when weeding. Feed veg., roses and some shrubs with organic fertilizer, also liquid seaweed. Remove bulb leaves when withered. Invite friends to supper and sit under honeysuckle as dew falls— heavenly smell! Watch blue tits using nest box. Sunset 22nd 9 p.m. (GMT 8 p.m.).

In kindergarten we had a list each month of what needed doing; it was satisfying to tick something off! There was always a lot to do but it was an essential part of the children's education and happiness. Some things had to be carried over to the following month! Here is a sample, also from May:

Move big logs. Water seeds. Plant out seedlings. Trim and weave willow tunnel. Move woodchips. Weed beds. Remove stick fence round bulbs. Fix wobbly hammock pole. Move compost heaps back. Cut overgrown bit behind window. Paint little house roof with preservative. Sort out path in front of little house. Cut old birch branch for hobby horses.

Tools and equipment (see Appendix 2)

Rowan, whose mother worked in a garden centre, spent many happy hours in his playgroup pushing his wheelbarrow about very carefully. It can be helpful to remember that imitation is strong in the young child, for if you set a good example in caring for tools and equipment they may develop such a habit too. Many children feel uncomfortable if things are out of time or place.

It is disheartening to have bent, rusty or broken equipment, so it is worth saving up to buy good quality. Your tools might include a trowel, spade, fork, hand fork, hoe, rake, wheelbarrow, watering can, bucket, trug basket, gloves and stiff broom. Keep spades sharp with a whetstone. You can use a piece of wood to scrape tools clean, a brush for washing them and an oily rag to prevent rust. Responsible children can be given a knife, secateurs and shears.

Compost, leaf mould and mulch

These bring smiles to the garden, returning to the ground what was taken from it: biodegradable, organic matter from prunings, weeds, kitchen waste, grass cuttings, leaves and dead flowers, transformed into friable soil.

29 January: Turn and tidy up compost heaps. Start carting finished compost to plants. Children to use barrows and trowels.

Compost and mulches are especially useful for very poor, heavy, light, dry or wet soils, aiding soil structure, resisting compaction and preventing erosion by holding water yet allowing drainage. Less watering is needed and roots can penetrate more easily, therefore plants survive and grow better. They provide valuable nutrients, trace elements and micro-organisms, many of which are not found in chemical additions. Are these not compelling reasons for making such composts and having a chemical-free garden for your children? Compost and leaf mould (just leaves) can be piled in wooden boxes, plastic bins, netting or just in a mound, best covered to keep the heat in, for instance under old rush matting or cardboard. One can use worn-out carpets, but unless they are *really* old it is hard to ensure they do not contain toxins. Some councils now ban carpets on allot-

Moving mulch with proper forks

ments due to the chemical residues

Giving compost to the roses

they may contain. Leaves left on beds help keep the ground warm over the winter, so one can wait until spring to add them to the leaf heap, where you will reap compost two years later (as leaves take longer to break down than other waste). Compost can take between six months and a year to form. Mulch is a thick layer of plant material or half-rotted compost put round plants. It controls weeds and prevents drying out by sun and wind. It will rot in time and become compost naturally. In Appendix 2 you will find information and books on composting from the Bio-Dynamic Agricultural Association, Garden Organic (Henry Doubleday Research Organization), Permaculture and Soil Association.

Please ask for alternatives to peat if you buy compost, as its collection is environmentally unfriendly. Peat has few nutrients and is home to rare plants and animals. It takes thousands of years to form.

Worms

In autumn, worms help clearing fallen leaves by pulling them into the ground, making them look like little sailing boats. Worms let air into the soil by tunnelling, so roots grow better and water is absorbed. Their casts are full of plant nutrients, being the waste of digested organic matter. Indoor worm bins use kitchen material, which can be used for indoor plants, ideal for those without a garden. Children like to rescue worms from wet roads. (Your council may have offers on worm and compost bins and water butts.)

Pests and diseases—environmentally friendly methods

1 October. Rake and scrape up new molehill earth, and spread on garden. (*Such earth is finely tilled by the moles and full of nutrients.*)

Gardening with wildlife in mind puts a different slant on the pest and disease troubles all gardeners encounter. Wherever you are there will be some creature which you would prefer to see elsewhere, yet many are the gardener's friend. Children should be as respectful as possible to whatever they see, so try to keep your thoughts to yourself about the earwigs that eat your apples and the caterpillars that devour the cabbages. They are just part of the food chain. The children can put grub-eaten apples or cabbage onto the compost heap so their earwigs and caterpillars can 'finish their meal'. If the heap gets hot enough, it should kill them. Sometimes moles uprooted our plants. Although we rarely saw one, we loved them, knowing they are soft and dear with their big shovelling feet. They eat grubs which would otherwise eat plants. Slugs dislike coffee grounds, ash or crushed egg or beach shells. Frogs and toads, encouraged by a pond, stones or rockery, eat slugs. Ladybird and lacewing houses are palaces for these aphid-devourers. Who does not love a ladybird crawling over one's hand? A pile of leaves or sticks is a cosy place for hedgehogs: slug and crunchy-bug vacuum cleaners. Earwigs, which eat your fruit, creep into upside-down flower pots filled with straw, so you can collect them to put somewhere else where they can do less damage. Spiders eat the flies we prefer not to have on our food. I knew an old lady who gently lifted the cobwebs, dusted underneath and then replaced them! Diluted bio-degradable washing-up liquid sprayed onto plants removes greenfly.

Crop rotation in the vegetable garden prevents transfer of pests and diseases, and some plants leave useful elements in the soil for the next crop. Peas and beans, for instance, should be cut off when they are finished, not pulled up, since they leave their nitrogen nodules in the ground. There are books on companion-planting, which is a way of strengthening plant resistance and deterring pests. Nasturtium, for instance, is popular with blackfly, thereby keeping it off other places. Physical protection such as fine mesh over certain plants plagued by unwanted insects and birds is practical, but it keeps out useful ones. Although children love cats and birds, it can be distressing when they scratch up seeds and young plants, so place prickly branches or wind black thread between upright twigs to keep them off. Chemicals destroy some of the life of a garden and use much energy in production and transport, besides which they get into our own food chain which research shows is unhealthy. The main thing is to have the garden as healthy as possible so plants can withstand and outlive troubles. There are many organic and biodynamic sprays and fertilizers for enhancing the life of the garden (see Appendix 2).

Pets and wildlife

A 6-year-old corrected his friend. 'No, tigers are scared of humans. But sometimes cats catch tigers.'

Caring for pets and wildlife helps children to develop sociability, responsibility and respect.

Children love collecting eggs from hens and feeding them. They don't mind cleaning them out if no one has said 'ugh'. You can buy hen food, and give them vegetable food scraps, cooked and raw, and even some plant cuttings. You will soon see what they like.

Children love cats and dogs. One of our cats came for walks with us. They lived in a shed where swallows nested but didn't catch any. They had enough rabbits, spiders and mice to eat. It is hard to make cats not catch birds. A bell tied round their neck enables birds to hear them coming. Care should of course be taken with dogs you don't know well...

One rainy day in kindergarten, we accompanied a local farmer who was giving us wood for our bread oven. We helped to load up the cart, then

Farm visit

On the farm

walked with him and his enormous black horse to the oven. After we had helped unload, we returned to the stable to brush and dry the horse. 'It's nice and warm in here,' said 4-year-old Charlotte, watching steam rising from the big animal. We fed him apples before we thanked the farmer and turned to wend our wet, weary but heart-warmed way home. It was a unique event which the children played out all that week. Farm visits can bring children similar adventures.

3 April: Expedition to the Gillmans to see lambs being fed. Break in their sitting room. Of course the children wanted to take the lambs home...

Happy children

Children are tickled by incidents like birds pulling up over-sized worms, struggling to fly away with their heavy load, or robins and blackbirds bravely alighting on your outdoor breakfast table for a few crumbs. Without wild creatures and wild places, human beings could not survive, for all living things are interdependent. Swallows and swifts swoop and squeal overhead for mosquito-supper, delighting the family with their speed and acrobatics. Half-grown frogs greet you amongst the plants. Newly flown tits twitter, quite unafraid, preening their new feathers and eating greenfly. Their voices change from tiny 'peep, peeps' to loud 'tweet, tweets' in the nest; nice for children to hear.

We encourage wild creatures by putting up nest boxes, leaving rough areas, giving water and ensuring there is food by not killing every unwanted thing in sight. You can hear the tap, tap, tap of thrushes breaking snail shells on a stone or step. Lizards like sunny stone walls. Butterflies particularly love buddleia, and bees love Michaelmas daisies. A comfrey or nettle patch is popular with various egg-laying butterflies. It makes fine compost, and fresh, new nettles make a fine soup. Children like bravely pinching the leaves quickly between their fingers and chopping them up, which destroys the stings. Yew berries are not good for us, but finches love them. Ladybirds, larvae, beetles, spiders and various minute creatures appreciate vegetable gardens, rock piles, compost heaps, tree stumps and roots. It is fascinating to lie in long grass or a scrubby area with a magnifying glass and observe the circus below: miniature beetles, ants, caterpillars and fat worms all moving between tiny plants. You may like to take the children to a nature reserve hide if they know how to keep quiet, to

Pile of rocks, also for play

watch birds and animals close by. Children can begin to use binoculars *properly* from about the age of 7. Listening in woods to birds and animals, you can guess what each rustling is in the undergrowth. Is a bird making cross noises in the tree, or is it a squirrel?

How many different habitats can you create for wildlife? Water, wild flowers, hedges, trees, decaying matter . . . the more there are, the greater the biodiversity. Mounting pressure on the countryside for building can be somewhat counteracted by creating joined-up wild areas for wildlife survival: a hedge between pond and pile of logs, a bramble bush between compost heap and orchard, a bank of nettles by a rotting shed or boggy place. Many footpaths and bridleways are bordered by verges, hedges and scrub, attractive to wild creatures. Rocks and stones in a pile make welcoming wildlife homes. A weedy lawn is full of biodiversity! You can turn part of it into a wildflower meadow, waiting to see what comes up and then adding what you like. It works better to plant seedlings than spread seed onto the lawn.

25–29 February: Pruning week if possible, two apple trees, roses, etc. Children help with rakes and barrows, taking prunings to stick pile. Some older ones can cut old flower stalks and small twigs with secateurs.

29 February. Review: Mostly lovely weather, lots done, children keen. Bit muddy, never mind. Great for mud pies and mole-tunnel hunts.

Bark texture

If there is room to leave part of a fallen branch or tree, it will provide much needed food and homes for wildlife. When people cut down trees, remove hedges, grub up heathland and drain ponds and ditches, they may declare there are plenty of other places for the wildlife to go, but other creatures already occupy those places. Living things live on untidy window sills: lichen, caterpillars, spiders, moss . . .

Children like to watch rabbits hopping across a field, frogs leaping into a pond or blue tits swinging about eating evening primrose seeds. Trees are havens for children as well as wildlife. They provide marvellous places to climb, swing, explore, hide, read, shelter, play and picnic. Children can run their hands over the bark or make bark rubbings. Trees are also planted to prevent soil erosion around the world.

Now winter is here
With snow and with sleet,
The poor little birds
Have nothing to eat.

I give them some crumbs,
They come with a rush,
The sparrow and robin
The wren and the thrush.

They come close beside me,
Their little hearts bold,
Their fear has all vanished
With hunger and cold.

Source unknown

Throughout winter, many plants provide homes and protection for invertebrates and insects, themselves food for other wildlife. Roundabouts and roadside verges can be havens for birds and animals. Unfortunately much wildlife loses its life on the roads. Squashed animals and birds are a sorry sight for children (and adults).

Ponds

Ponds are rewarding for people and wildlife. Pond-dipping with nets and sieves is a favourite activity for children. Our kindergarten children loved feeling slimy frogspawn and gazing in to see water skaters, newts and tadpoles, with the odd surprise of a frog leaping in from under a stone. Yellow iris, water forget-me-not, water mint and water lilies shelter creatures below. In winter, ponds are quite different; everything has gone to sleep and ice makes a blanket. It is good to keep a patch open for wild creatures. Water birds swim to keep a place open until the cold freezes it over altogether.

Birds

At kindergarten break we had a crumb plate onto which any fallen grains and crumbs could feed the birds. You can do this at home too, of course. Sometimes children brought a basket of autumn berries for the birds. They threaded peanuts in their shells and dried pumpkin seeds to hang up. In winter, birds like apple and pear pieces. Children can chop apples, cheese and bacon rinds. Try mixing birdseed, oatmeal, nuts and dried fruit into warm melted fat (under supervision), then fill half-coconuts to hang upside-down.

Different birds choose different homes: eaves, untidy shrubs, sheds, rushes, undergrowth, caves, cliffs, shingle, climbing plants, trees, nest boxes. They need a variety of nesting material, such as mud, moss, feathers, twigs and leaves. The long-tailed tit builds a marvel from lichen, moss and cobwebs. In spring, leave out sheep's wool and your children's cut hair. They will be proud if it disappears. They must be discouraged from picking up fallen baby birds; the parents abandon them if touched.

Birds drink, wash and preen their feathers in a birdbath, or an old dustbin lid upside-down on the ground. Put big stones in deep baths so birds cannot drown. Place bird feeders, tables and baths where birds can escape potential danger. Ensure they are kept clean. When your pond is frozen, place a pan of hot water on the ice to melt it so birds can drink. (Smashing it can kill small creatures through shock waves.)

In summary

Supporting wildlife, caring for animals and tending a garden is a gift for children's body and soul, and kindles their growing imagination and activity. In the next chapter we shall see how outdoor design can further enhance children's well-being.

9
OUTDOOR DESIGN AND CREATION

A wealth of different places

'I just want to explore!' said an educational consultant visiting a pre-school garden, when she was supposed to be leading a meeting. If an adult was so moved in this way, one can imagine how it was for a child. Nelly, in hospital for a brief spell, talked about her life as a farmer's wife and how she was looking forward to getting back to work in her garden. She walked about the ward, bright and clear-headed, then sat down to read the latest news. She was 98. It has often struck me how people who spend much time outside seem to have a particular quality of bodily and spiritual health. Is this not a winning argument for offering children great outdoor opportunities?

An old man remarked on the 'riot of colour' in a higgledy-piggledy suburban garden: 'This is how a garden should be,' said a landscape gardener. Visiting children explored that half-wild, half-tamed, secret garden along its curving path amongst tall plants. Roses, honeysuckle and hollyhocks grew up the walls in summer, while winter honeysuckle and jasmine filled the surroundings with scent at the dark time of the year. The whole garden fitted into a space 5 by 8 metres.

Toys such as yo-yos, jacks and elastics (long pieces of elastic round the ankles of two children for jumping in neat and contorted ways) become all the rage from time to time, especially where children play together outdoors after school. Children naturally form groups and friendly-hostile gangs in mid-childhood, needing time and space to play out these dynamics in wild or intelligently designed areas. Gangs are more likely to die away if young people grow through uncertainty and insecurity to a sense of individuality and responsibility. Ventures such as the BBC's 'Breathing Places' involve local people creating green spaces where people work, go to school and live. Traffic-calming makes areas for sociable interaction. Tiddlywinks, four square, and hopscotch can be played in child-friendly streets in imaginatively designed estates. Children have the chance to be outdoors more when we distance ourselves from the overwhelming climate of fear. Remembering that trust is a vital ingredient of childhood, we can return to looser rules and less supervision. 'Be home by six and don't go down Shivers Lane.' Children obey if they know they will not be allowed out again otherwise. Children respect freedom within boundaries.

Design

A good design with a sense of movement helps one to breathe and relax. It need not be formal or fancy; just feel comfortable and comfort your soul. When dreaming up your wonderful space, think about what the children and you want to *do* in it. Children want to run, jump, get lost, play games, climb, skip and chat. These thoughts will inspire you, so that what you want to have in your space will become obvious. If you aim for the best possible of what you want, you are halfway there. If you get bogged down in affordability, detail, and health and safety you won't get very far. Just aim to do the best that is possible!

One can use a bit of imagination and psychology in seeing what the children want to *have*, translating it into what they want to *do*. They know what they have experienced but cannot express thoughts analytically for some years; this needs more developed conceptualization. For example, children say 'I want a maze,' because they had fun in the Hampton Court or maize field ones. Actually they really enjoyed wandering about and getting lost, so you can see what you can do to make this possible. A mini-wilderness or collection of different spaces might fit the bill. That would all give lots to *do* without *having* so much in their unplanned space. If you want an actual maze, it would not need to be very specific like a circle or squared pattern: haphazard is more fun. The height is not so important for younger children: you can get 'lost' amongst plants a foot high! It could be a maze of vegetables and flowers, or more permanent hedging. What about one on a hill or slope, for added thrills? Or: 'We want to play football!' Do they need a pitch, or would an open space do where they can play other things as well? 'We want to tell each other stories so we want a seat.' This may have been their experience, yet you can expand it for them by thinking about what they will be *doing*; so *having* pieces of branch, steps and random walls to sit on facilitates storytelling, but can also extend into all sorts of other activities as well.

Many children need calming down after being in a poorly designed playground. Maybe there is tarmac, plastic and metal rather than earth, grass and wood. Perhaps there are only representational playthings, nowhere to hide, few plants and bare walls. In chapter 4 I wrote about open-ended, non-representational playthings and equipment. I want to say the same again about the whole space where children play and work. Think of a wood, hillside or unkempt outdoor space: what imaginative realms can open up in a non-specified, open-ended natural setting!

A space growing slowly and organically invites reflection and ongoing creativity. Being in a constant state of growth and change, landscapes are never finished. Trees die, cliffs erode, plants disappear. Outdoors is more transformable than a building, which needs to be solid from the start. Even if it grows slowly, an imaginatively designed outdoor space helps to create harmony amongst children. In educational establishments, parents like to be kept informed and consulted. Will it be mapped out on paper or computer? Perhaps nothing will be written; conversations will be enough. When something has been achieved, have a party!

It is excellent to involve the children. They may know what they want but be unable to visualize anything beyond the familiar. When they ask for a slide, they may mean they want to rush downhill. A see-saw, swing, steep slope or rope from a tree might fit the bill. Wanting a jungle trail could mean scrambling around at all angles, like on logs, ropes, ladders or lying branches. I know a prep school with a wild patch of trees and bushes which they call the 'jungle'. Children definitely want the opportunity for safe and more challenging risk-taking, as I have often observed. It was fascinating to see how certain children cried if stung unexpectedly by a nettle, yet walk self-initiated into our nettle bed.

It is good to balance rough, wild parts and more contained places, or muddy and clean areas. Dancing, hiding, construction, exploration and quiet solace need room yet can be made in a surprisingly small space. Children like to move things such as benches and logs to create new worlds. It is good to have a certain amount of grass for play and also for class or family picnics, and hard surfaces for certain games. Really old carpet on some rough land opened up for play will soon become green but not allow growth from underneath for some time.

Steps, slopes and paths connect different parts of the outdoor space. Focal points may be special seating, a paved surface for skipping, ball and other games, or a sandpit. Paths to an open air stage invite transition to a different world. It can be something else when not being used for drama.

As part of a school's design process, my son Mark, landscape architect, likes to spend some hours with the children so they can get to know him, then tell, draw and write what they would like. He plays imaginative games on their playground, running across invisible bridges, climbing fantasy trees and creeping into tiny unseen houses. The children warm up and respond excitedly as he kindles their imagination. Knowing that younger ones cannot grasp abstract ideas, he takes groups of 4-, 5- or 6-year-olds on an adventure, telling them a story with corresponding actions, moving about all over the tarmac. Gradually their imitative nature and interest lead them to copy him. Afterwards the children really look forward to their house, garden, sandy 'beach', pond, wood or whatever. Below is a *very* brief summary of one story, with just three descriptions *(in italics)* of the many actions involved, as examples.

Once upon a time, a storm blew up near the sea. It knocked trees and houses over, so everyone moved away. The storm left a wide sandy beach which people came to enjoy. A wide car park was built *(brrrm, 'cars' driving about)*. The sand washed away until the beach was rocky again and everyone left. A poor family made a shelter on the hard, cracked car park, using driftwood and fallen trees. Birds brought moss and soft leaves for beds. The grateful family found a dustbin lid for a bird bath. Fairies saw the ugly car park and blew dandelion seeds into the cracks. Dandelions made pretty yellow winding rows. Squirrels buried their nuts in the cracks but forgot where, so trees started to grow. Dwarves jumped up and down amongst the trees, jumping a big hole in the ground *(jumping)*. Clouds rained it full. This new pond was by the family's shelter so they built a bridge across it *(balance across 'bridge')*. Frogs and pond skaters came to live in it. The family made benches and fences, laid paths and dug up the car park for a vegetable and flower garden and an orchard. They collected rocks from the beach for a proper house. They harvested vegetables and fruit and decorated with roses, then invited people to celebrate. Everyone danced and ate a big vegetable stew. And they all lived happily ever after.

Older children can design in other hands-on ways. For instance, Mark took a class of 8- and 9-year-olds onto the playground and asked if they would prefer an orchard or a wood. They chose an orchard. 'How should it be: in rows or planted randomly?' he asked. They decided on rows. 'Let's stand in the imaginary rows,' he said, so they did. 'Now let's stand randomly.' They decided they would have their orchard with trees growing randomly here and there. Their actual experience had spoken, because they were involved rather than just consulted.

Beginning the playground story

Making 'stew' in playground story

Responding to the landscape

What might become of this low corner, those yet small trees or that neglected hedge? Should this patch be cultivated, that unproductive vegetable bed become a wild space? If this area leads to a dead end, what is there of interest at that point? Recognizing that curiosity, interest, wonder, excitement and joy are of paramount importance in childhood will help us to make the utmost of our space.

Imaginative ideas can arise through following the natural contours of the landscape. Varied land shapes offer opportunity for movement and orientation skills. A mound or hill offers differentiation in gradient, height and depth, especially if broken up by varying levels and steps. Slopes and shapes may come about naturally; digging a large dip, for example, provides soil and turf for building a curving bank. Perhaps each area leads to the next quite naturally; otherwise this can be incorporated into the design. You may want to gradually plant an orchard or wood if you have room. One can make flower or vegetable beds on a slope by creating terraces. Beds on the flat can

Terraced hill in spring

have interesting shapes. If alongside a wall, they might be curved or zigzag, perhaps with seating in the curving parts. Beds without straight edges enable more children to work in them at once. See how your landscape 'speaks' to you before embarking on any ideas. In a school, you may want to put money aside for professional design guidance.

Weather

Where is the sun and how long does it shine in which parts of your space? There may be corners that barely or never see the sun. Where is the prevailing wind and how strong is it generally? How much rainfall and cloud cover is there? When is frost likely? You may need to design protection from excessive rain, sun, cold and wind.

Soil

The geology of your area may present clay, rock, sand or a fine loam. Perhaps topsoil was removed in a new space. You may have a rich, worm and humus-filled earth full of micro-organisms, or soil that has been denuded by monoculture and chemical treatments, needing humus and natural soil improvers. You might drain sodden ground by making ditches, or have a bog garden. Draining is suitable only in carefully thought-out small areas, as draining in larger ones can contribute to flooding in other areas.

N.B. *Make sure you know where the drains, water, gas and electricity pipes, cable TV and telephone cables are before doing more than modest digging.*

The area

Is it urban or rural, pleasant or deprived? I really think that disadvantaged places should be given priority by councils. Poorer areas tend to have grass 'deserts' with little focus, where people are afraid to go. Public playgrounds are often fenced in and only younger children allowed. There are ways of making things vandal-proof, but if spaces are designed and built involving young people's ideas and help, they are more likely to work. There is evidence of crime reduction in well-designed places: soul-fulfilling rather than soul-destroying. Thoughtful developers ensure people have access to individual or shared gardens and public transport to larger gardens and parks. City community gardens are splendid for getting families together.

The UK Early Years' Framework states: 'Wherever possible, there should be access to an outdoor play area...'

Execution

13 May: Work-experience students digging new sandpit outside Zsuzsa's class. Exciting!

15 June: Year 10 from 'Big School' digging and building patio next door. We watched them on 'television' (i.e. through window!).

Children and young people appreciate being involved in creating or changing part of a garden or playground. Older children like constructing something for others: a playhouse, posts for a hammock, walls, a pond, a waterfall, hedges ... I have experienced all this in 8- to 18-year-olds.

7 May: Helped Class 9 transporting bricks up hill to bread oven site. Great experience, do it again.

8 May: More transporting.

9 May: More transporting.

Young children can help at home or school: carrying bricks, wheeling soil or woodchips about, setting stones, digging for drains or shoring up edges. Older children or adults working are a marvellous image for little ones. Enthusiastic, willing parents, staff and friends are rewarded by the children's happiness. Workdays are fun and great social occasions: entertaining, exhausting, adventurous, inspiring, embracing, exciting—and so worthwhile.

People can get carried away with their design and then become disheartened as it is all too much, or they find that it has not worked. For example, a spiral path was laboriously made up a hill, but the children just made their own path straight up, getting muddy rolling down! It is better to give volunteers a rough outline rather than have them do the large overall design. If they have a sketched plan, they can just take off. Hang it on a wall, so people can stick post-it notes on about additional ideas or what they can offer. In this way one can incorporate their enthusiasm and generosity. One might need to say, 'No, thanks,' but one should not be too fixed. 'I can build a wall!'—'Great, we could have one there!'—'Well, that's where we thought of putting a pile of logs, so perhaps here.'—'Maybe we don't need a bench there after all, we could sit on your wall and spend the money on something else!'

Are ideas about subsequent maintenance realistic? Who will maintain the garden, keep paths swept and benches clean? Grass and weeds wait for no one. Manfred said of his fancy new garden, 'She designed it, but I have to look after it.' Children involved in caring for their surroundings translate this inwardly into self-care and respect for others.

Much is possible with little money. The less sophisticated and cheaper projects are often more effective. Much depends on how much help there is. Family and friends may be happy to help in your garden. Grants are available (see Appendix 2).

Lay people often have inspirational and imaginative vision, yet landscape architects, who also plan 50 years ahead, know how to put ideas together so that they work and become reality now. If you have enough cash and no time, you could pay lots of money for good professionals to design and build your space; it will be lovely and you will have no problems. Otherwise you may have a perfect garden or playground in 20 years' time, slowly achieving it by trial and error and scrapping bits that don't work and trying again.

Seating

Who and what is your seating for? For parents to wait and chat, perhaps under cover and near pretty and sweet-smelling plants? For children to play grown-ups (or 'children'), or a thousand other games of the imagination? As I have already written, anything offered with children and play in mind is wonderful if open-ended, so please keep this in mind with your seats. Places specifically meant for sitting (benches of some sort) can have interesting shapes, for instance following the contours of buildings, built around a tree, beneath an arch or curved by a winding hedge. They could be large or very small, adding to scope for games. Any place for sitting may be in noisy, busy areas or quiet ones. It is good to have a variety of different kinds in different places. Low walls, raised-bed edging, steps, branches and logs can double for seating and play. Children just sit wherever is handy, including the ground. Naturally one does not want muddy feet on 'proper' seats (benches), so make a rule that dirty footwear must be removed on them. Children appreciate logs by a sandpit or 'quarry', valuable also when adults are invited to a sand tea party.

New playground beginnings with diminishing willow tunnel

Bench in the Ashdown Forest

Seating material should be durable, not take long to dry and not need much maintenance. *Metal* dries quickly but can feel, or actually *be*, too cold or hot. Depending on the material, it may become rusty. *Concrete* can be moulded into shapes and is maintenance free but cold, and may be rough or

Table and benches in Royal Botanical Gardens, Kew, at Wakehurst Place

*Bench on National
Cycle Path*

crumble away in frost. *Stone* can be sculpted into beautiful forms and is particularly suited to a warmer climate. *Plastic* dries quickly and is light and portable. Nevertheless, it may have a short life and be easily damaged. Recycled plastic-wood composite is low maintenance and durable. *Wood* is warm and can be very durable; it may remain damp in a wet season. It can be painted (and re-painted), but personally I like its own appearance, especially for children. If seasoned too quickly, it may split or warp. Hardwood is expensive but it lasts and does not need treating. It is worth looking locally

Oiling new bench

Log slices for sitting and fun

for a craftsman who makes beautiful benches straight from a trunk or branch. It is special if children's parents or their school make them. Slices of thick branch or tree trunk also serve well as seats (or imaginary boats, supermarkets, castles, mountains...).

Borders

A large grassy space may make children feel lost, so it wants an enfolding gesture with attractive edges. Unless it is needed for large games, boundaries

Log border, also for play

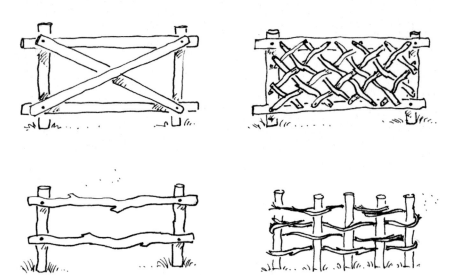

Fence sections of branches and twigs

break it into smaller, friendlier parts. Wind, noise or road-pollution barriers may be necessary. Any space for children needs the protection of borders. One can drive posts of varying diameters into the ground, close-to or apart, in winding shapes to make borders. Branches or prunings can be woven through to decorate them. Fruit trees can be trained into space-saving espaliers on walls or fences.

A circle of logs set upright into the ground becomes a place for play, story and picnic, completed by woodchips on a permeable membrane, carpet or cardboard. Peeling the bark off the ends to be buried and burning their surface deters rot. Logs of varying thickness and height dug into the ground enable balancing or weaving around. Narrow logs make the going more challenging. The boundary of a 'Treasure Island' might be composed of upright logs or horizontal ones held in place by short pegs.

Parents' Workday, digging-in circle of logs

Filling the log circle with wood chips

Log circle still good some years later after much use

Hedges

These are more user-friendly than solid fences, although one can grow climbers up the latter. They are better wind-barriers than walls or fences, which may create eddies. We had a hedge in kindergarten which was a superb place for play. We kept it cut to about 8 feet high and cut out some of the inner twigs. Children could really be on top of the world on it. Sometimes someone got stuck, but there was always a child or adult around to help. Holes in hedges make nooks for play; branches can be trained by tying together. A child-height hedge is fun to peep over. Adolescents enjoy hedge-laying: untidy old bushes and small trees are partially cut at the base, leant over and interwoven. New growth soon forms a beautiful, impenetrable hedge.

A quick way of making a hedge where you want a real fence is by planting a 'fedge': closely planted willow saplings.

Walls

These provide noise and road-pollution barriers, and create boundaries and play equipment (good for hiding and being private). With hooks, ropes and

Fun in the hedge

hand-holds they become mountains. Children like to walk along, jump off and sit on brick or stone walls.

Lewis described climbing onto a wall 1 metre high to take photos of a class. They gasped, 'That's dangerous!' Yet Felix, 4, used to clambering and leaping around, scrambled onto a wall 80 cm high, saying, 'Do you dare me to jump off here?' 'Yes,' I said. 'I'll just wait till that lady's gone past,' he said, then flew gracefully onto the pavement, totally in control, and practising spatial orientation, courage and self-esteem.

If a wall is to hold back earth, it should be thicker towards the bottom to hold the pressure. Leave small gaps in a low wall for plants and drainage. All retaining walls need 'weep holes'. They can just be the gaps between bricks or slabs (or proper holes in concrete). Water presses through them, draining from the top. Plant and animal life soon make their way into these gaps and holes. Slopes can be retained in a variety of ways, but this may be an engineering job, so consult someone with experience.

The ground

A variety of textures underfoot enhances movement and the senses. Uneven surfaces stretch physical skills and encourage imagination. Many children think earth was created for digging, so appreciate trenches and somewhere for muddy play.

Safety surfaces

A natural surface, such as wood chip, sand, grass, soil or undergrowth, is wonderful, so children can really get 'stuck in'. Manufactured matting is expensive to lay, wears out, and is not interactive: the mind is not encouraged to do anything else on it. Designs on the surfacing do not leave the children free in their imagination. If, for example, you have a recycled rubber play-surface, consider simple, natural tones; many types are available.

Log edging for wood chip

Drainage and ground cover

If you need a hard surface, for instance for a netball court or car park, can it be permeable? Some flooding is caused by not allowing water to follow its natural course or sink into the ground. Various structures allow drainage, such as a hexagonal plastic or concrete framework, allowing cars to drive over but greenery to grow through. Similar safety matting is available.

Bricks and paving laid with gaps have a rain-absorbing function; sand between hinders weeds. Water-absorbing rolls of turf are easier than sowing grass seed and not expensive. Pre-seeded grass matting of coir fibre for inclines stabilizes slopes until grass grows, then rots away. Bushes and small trees help steady it. Turf wears down with much footwork, but hard-wearing varieties are available. Grass is better not cut too short before the winter; it provides shelter for small creatures and keeps the ground warmer. There are artificial turfs to fill with sand—hard-wearing, right for sports and easy on the knees. Those without a rubber crumb underlay are best for ball bouncing.

Softwood decking is often treated with toxic chemicals. Sustainably sourced hardwood, such as oak, larch or chestnut, lasts and weathers better than softwood.

There are many pretty creeping plants for living ground cover.

Mosaic

Children, parents and teachers can design a very beautiful mosaic. It might be several square yards, or just small. Bricks, cobbles and broken pieces of slate, bathroom tiles or mirrors, pebbles and shells: families, friends and tile manufacturers may willingly provide the wherewithal. It will need to slope slightly and have drainage. Children love to help mix cement for laying the mosaic pieces. They can create pictures or patterns in the following way. Put tile pieces close together upside down in old trays. Spread cement over them, filling the tray. When dry and hard (a few days), turn the whole upside down and see what pretty thing has appeared. Integrate them whole into the mosaic. A mosaic compass is striking. Of course mosaics can decorate walls too. (See also Plates 5–8.)

Underground

Being underground develops courage. A post- and board-supported dugout in a bank is exciting and secret. A large pipe from a builder's

Preparing cement for mosaic

Mosaic-making with all ages

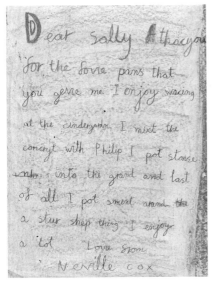

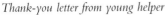

Thank-you letter from young helper

Quarry with pulleys

yard or reclamation centre can be covered with earth and turf from somewhere you are replacing. If your garden or playground is large enough, you could have a shallow 'quarry'. Children love digging down to nowhere in particular. A board surround and ladder for access with ropes, pulleys and buckets makes for hours of 'un-adult-erated' social and physical fun.

Painted forms and drawing

Hopscotch, Four square, Snakes and Ladders, etc. can be drawn with chalk or marked with sticks, rather than the permanent kind which 'fix' the area into a specific template. Children like to draw pictures and write cheeky words on the ground, but that is part of growing up. Rain or running feet will erase them. I have seen charmingly wobbly hopscotch drawn right up to 100. If compass points are painted onto concrete in a school, the names of countries the children and staff come from can be continually added—a celebration of cultural diversity. A wall for graffiti in the school playground allows artistic creations. Large shapes of outdoor plywood painted with blackboard paint and attached to a wall make an excellent easel. Chalks can be kept in a rainproof tin attached to the wall.

Paths

Enticing path

Following mysterious paths is magical. Meandering through tall vegetation, one could end at a glade, seat or vegetable garden. A trail of planks or stepping stones across a marshy area arouses curiosity. Straight paths are functional but have no dynamic possibilities.

Paths can be laid of brick in patterns, cobbles, stones, crazy paving or gravel. Laying paving or brick on the diagonal or in a fan creates an illusion of space. Recycled, environmentally-friendly Welsh blue slate chip is fairly expensive but attractive, durable, dry, clean and sustainable.

To prepare for path-laying, beat the soil down, possibly with smashed up rubble (great work for teenagers). A liner such as layers of cardboard (which don't last long) or permeable membrane is essential under wood chips to

Brick path-laying

Brick slope

prevent mixing with mud. Tree surgeons can provide 'woodland chips', cheaper than by the bag (they need to get rid of it). It may be leaves, twigs, bark and wood mixed up but makes fragrant paths. When it eventually rots, it can be used as mulch and replaced. Oak slabs at intervals along wood chip makes the going interesting, as do stepping stones in grass (set slightly lower for mowing over). Wire netting attached to each oak slab prevents slipping when wet, but we left them 'bare' in kindergarten as a balance challenge; the children didn't slip.

Bridges

Crossing a bridge takes children into another realm. A contoured one enables ascent and descent. It does not matter what is underneath: a stream, ditch or grassy trail.

A bridge or jetty enables children to examine a pond without slipping. They enjoy pond-dipping with nets or looking for 'water boatmen' and other delights. Our above-mentioned kindergarten 'river' (a 20-cm-deep ditch) was crossed by a hanging, moving bridge just 1 metre long, with a rope

Natural 'bridge' for play in country park

either side. It filled after much rain but there was always an adult about. The bridge was a favourite place to make a wobbly crossing or kneel to look for frogs and get wet hair.

To make a swing bridge, saw planks or poles the width of the proposed bridge, enough for a concave form. Drill horizontal holes for strong rope through the plank ends, the base of four strong posts and the top of the posts for the rope handrail. Set the posts in concrete at an angle away from the bridge. Thread the rope through the planks or poles and post bases (not too tightly to allow for wood expansion when wet, or with a knot between each). Make a solid knot the other side of the posts. Thread the handrails through and tie knots at each end.

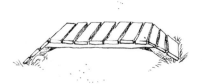
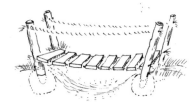

Bridges

Steps

Steps tied into wall and built leaning inwards for stability

These may be of stone, paving slabs, brick or roughly hewn rocks. They could be of turf, pebbles, earth or sand contained within wooden or brick risers; the wood is held in place by pegs driven into the ground.

Uneven steps of irregular heights, mimicking the unpredictability of nature, offer opportunities for spatial development, like climbing a natural hill. Placing steps at random where they are not actually needed fosters incentive and imaginative activity. (A piece of wall, short hedge, archway or seat in an unexpected place does the same.)

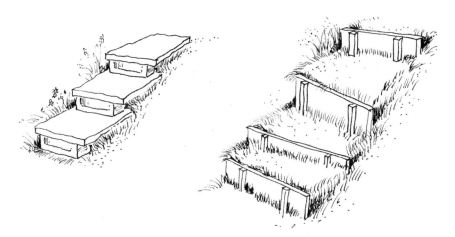

Examples of steps, even and uneven

Water and ponds

Children play in any puddle if given half a chance, and love to dam a ditch or stream. A hand pump with plastic guttering and buckets presents such joyful opportunities. A fountain or little stream is a real joy. A contrasting mixture of water, rocks and greenery is pleasing to the eye and heart. Seats near water offer interest, rest and reflection. I wrote many notes for this book by our small pond.

A 'flowform' mimics naturally falling water, cleansing and bringing life into it (see book by John Wilkes in Appendix 2). A series of little pools of rocks or waterproof cement keeps the water aerated and sounds beautiful. Life-bringing fountains, artificial streams and trickles make interesting noises and movements. I prefer a simple fountain for children (there is already plenty of decoration from plants). Buy a pump for low voltage (24V) to avoid a shock, and attach it to the same RCD (residual current device, for extra safety) that you hopefully have in your home or educational establishment. If the amount of energy required is small and there is no danger of theft or vandalism, you may be able to use a solar-powered pump. Ask at your aquatic centre. Clean the pump regularly and store it indoors over winter if the water is likely to freeze.

Preserving Children	
	Into field pour children and dogs
1 grass field	*Allow to mix well*
1 dozen children	*Pour brook over pebbles until slightly frothy*
1 brook	*When children are nicely brown, cool off in pebble froth*
1 hundredweight of pebbles	*When dry, serve with hot milk and freshly baked*
½ dozen dogs (and puppies if *available)*	*gingerbread*
	Old recipe

Pond-building

In heavy clay one can have a natural pool if the water table is high enough: children enjoy digging a hole and seeing if it fills. Prefabricated shapes can look natural once plants take over. A butyl (artificial rubber) liner allows for individuality; try out different shapes with string on the surface before digging. Dug-out earth could make a hill for a waterfall. Once the hole is dug, remove stones and ram it down by stamping and jumping (special entertainment). Put in 10 cm of sand to stop damage to the liner. Make different levels for planted-up earth or pots, in steps to avoid collapsing. Smooth the liner in and cut off the top, leaving about 20 cm over the edge; a handy job for eager children. Lay bricks, soil or rocks over it to keep it in place. *If buying rocks for your pond, please ensure they are not limestone pavement or other rare resource, nor transported across the world.* A soil edge will become marshy, good for bog plants. It looks charming if rough grass, stones and plants flop over the edge, allowing birds to bathe, hedgehogs to drink and frogs to hide. It is best to wait for the rain to fill it. Add a couple of bucketfuls from an established pond for micro-life, especially if you fill it with tap-water. Then wait for wildlife to appear. The pond may nearly dry out in summer, but this does not matter so long as there is a little left; this happens in nature too. The roots on the sides will draw up water from the bottom. Top it up with rainwater if possible, which is better for the pond and not stressful for reservoirs and rivers. Besides using water butts, it is fun to leave buckets out to see how much they fill with rainwater. Rotting vegetation encourages algal growth so needs removing. Children can help thin out excess plants, prising thick roots apart or slicing through them with a big knife (best done in early autumn to allow plants to re-establish and avoid disturbance to hibernating creatures or to tadpoles in spring). Fish add nutrients and eat invertebrates, so a balance will have to be found if children want fish. If much of the surface is covered, for instance by water lilies, there is less trouble from algae. Water snails and oxygenating plants help keep the water clear. Dragonflies like some open water. Where needed, a safety grid from a garden centre or blacksmith can cover a pond just under the surface, with lockable opening lids for investigation.

Some ponds are too big to cover. Fences may be ugly and are not always reliably safe. In every case with water, wherever it is and whatever the size or depth, vigilance is the best safety net with younger children. Teaching safety to children old enough to know what they are doing is the best policy.

Small pools

A shallow area of paving filled with water or a fountain in a dish with a few pebbles is pleasing for little children. They like pouring water in, splashing and paddling. With a slope by it, a pump could move the water round and down the incline. An old sink needs supervision; float wood in it for small creatures to climb on to avoid drowning. For a miniature raised pond, build a surrounding wall, say 100 cm long by 30 wide by 30 deep. Put 10 cm of sand in the bottom and line it with pond rubber, leaving some hanging over the top. Put a layer of the wall material over that, giving it a key by cutting gaps in the rubber. Cut off the excess. With large stones in it, drowning is a near impossibility for birds, frogs or children.

Children love wobbling about in this song:

Three ducks on a pond, wibble, wobble, wibble, wobble,
Three ducks on a pond, wibble, wobble, wibble, wobble,
Three old women, going to market, wibble, wibble, wobble—wibble, wibble, wobble.

Anon

Pond plants

Choose non-invasive, native plants. Water lilies, irises, water forget-me-not, mint and kingcups are lovely. Hemerocallis (day lily), candelabra primulas, astilbe and creeping jenny are attractive at the edge.

Fireplace

Fire cannot spread so easily outside a circle of bricks or rocks, which make a boundary, not least for children to respect.

Children can tend the fire and hold sticks with food over it. Logs or planks for sitting around the fireplace also mark a boundary. Wood for the indoor or outdoor fire can be sawn, chopped and stacked neatly with the children. A wooden roof or tarpaulin tied down enables rain to drain away. Stacking between two trees or four upright posts is attractive.

Fireplace in the making

Small or awkward spaces

Many gardens and playgrounds are small and have traffic going by. A high fence or bank of earth to ward off noise and fumes could be covered with plants. Some playgrounds have a hard surface which may not be dug up, but tubs, sinks or raised beds for climbers and small trees can be stood on it. It could be covered with wood chips or sand-filled artificial grass.

Old carpet could cover some of a muddy area, leaving some for play. Paving or decking can cover some ground as a practical measure. Gravel, wood chips and wood slabs could lie on top, with paraphernalia for a 'Treasure Island'. A circle of logs would make a friendly corner or border for a sandpit. Attaching ropes or the washing line to fences or walls provides a frame for a tent of cloths and a happy game. We once squeezed our tent onto someone's pocket-handkerchief lawn for us all to sleep in.

Small flower and vegetable beds improve a miniature area. What about a two-tiered garden? A two-storey, narrow playhouse or tower could be one side. One can build a platform for extra play space, with (securely fixed) plants in tubs on it (sun-loving) and below (shade-loving). Different levels also give additional space for adults. For a vegetable bed containing courgettes, cucumbers and/or tomatoes, sink posts into the ground, leaving 2 metres above the ground. Tie wires between the posts 2 metres high, and train the afore-mentioned plants up the posts and along the wires. The plants 'downstairs' need enough light and sun from the side and between the plants 'upstairs', so make sure there are gaps between the latter.

Roof gardens

What fun, how exciting and beautiful to see out so far and feel one can breathe! Roof gardens are insulating and soak up water which otherwise enters drains. Some modern architects are taking increased flooding into consideration and so incorporating roof gardens.

Trees can be grown as well as lawns and vegetable plots, providing a habitat for wildlife. I have seen *large* trees growing on fourth and fifth floors, though where the roots went is a mystery I was unable to fathom (possibly into brickwork, which would be structurally dangerous!). Some school playgrounds are on roofs if space is at a premium—exhilarating! Wind and sun may cause problems, so shady plantings or windbreaks are needed. Garage roofs lend themselves to gardens.

Consult a structural engineer before embarking on a roof garden: how much weight can it carry, is it waterproof and is planning permission needed? Roof-garden experts advise on suitability of weather and climate, water retention and drainage, wind and sun protection, appropriate soils, plants, erection of trellis or walls and sturdy but lightweight containers. It can be complicated and expensive to create a roof garden on an existing building, whereas integrating one in a new building is more straightforward. Perhaps make a turf roof on a flat-roofed shed or playhouse—not so heavy, nor drastic if it leaks.

Indoor gardens

For a rock or water garden indoors, fill a plastic sandpit with soil, plant flowers and salads in it, or make a boggy area with water plants. Shade-loving plants are suitable for indoor planting. Children in wheelchairs will enjoy watering and caring for pots on a deep, wide shelf and looking after animals such as rabbits or guinea pigs on a raised surface.

Allotments

Many city folk spend many a happy day on their allotment, away from buzz and bustle whilst enjoying fresh air and food. Some people make their toolshed into an attractive day-home, or leave room for a swing and mini-lawn for play and picnics.

Water may have to be carried from a standpipe but children can help carry watering cans. Allotment rents are low because councils support people's health and 'growing their own'. If they have been abandoned for a while, it is wise to tackle a small patch at a time, mowing the parts not yet in use. Some people manage to make regular trips to their allotment garden which is especially beneficial for city children. Several nurseries and schools with limited space have allotments, even in city playgrounds. Various socially aware and environmentally minded groups clear rough areas in cities for a range of habitats and community allotments.

Window sills and balconies

We have grown sweet peas, lettuces and herbs all squashed together on a window sill, making the rooms and outside of the building look pretty whilst making us feel self-sufficient!

You can make window boxes of recycled wood. All boxes and pots need drainage holes and pieces of wood or brick underneath for air circulation, with stones or broken crocks at the bottom. Protect plants from hot sun by putting their pots into an extra container or rigging up shade. They appreciate an evening spray of water in hot weather; daytime watering can scald them. Naturally everything must be securely held so there is no danger of falling.

Small bulbs are charming in window boxes, such as chionodoxa, scilla, snowdrops, crocus, small tulips and narcissi. They leave room for other plants and can be left in from year to year. Pelargoniums (zonal geraniums), herbs, alpine strawberries, sweet peas, spring onions, radishes and salads grow well in this mini-garden. Sow seeds directly into boxes or pots, or buy plants if you prefer. Keep birds and cats off by winding black thread between sticks. Organic compost holds water and feeds the plants. Although plants must be kept damp (with rainwater if possible), children should not be over-zealous, as plants may 'drown' and decay. Many people have balconies of pretty plants and small trees, even at the top of high-rise buildings. Such environments add so much to everyone's well-being.

Vandalism and reaching out to young people

Many settings and schools are prey to vandalism, particularly in cities. It has been found that the more attractive the setting, the less vulnerable it is. If colleagues and parents do not become disheartened but keep putting everything to rights again, vandalism may diminish as the perpetrators give up. Preferably get them to help if you know who they are!

Using school grounds in the evenings adds to local amenities and reduces trouble, particularly when the young people have been involved in creating facilities. Whenever the community is involved, people feel responsible and take care. Movable equipment can be brought inside or locked up. If bricks, large pieces of wood, etc. cause problems left outside, a daily exercise could be to wheel them out on barrows and carts and bring them in again.

If parks are well kept and a warden is on duty, they should be safe and clean for everyone. Babies and parents, children, grandparents and football fans all use them, especially important for those without gardens. Sherrie's kindergarten had no playground but access to a pretty corner of a park. Early every morning she donned thick gloves and combed it for litter, cigarette ends, broken glass and needles. The council removed graffiti from time to time. Through her devoted efforts she made daily play possible there. A town in the north of England was the scene of riots some years ago; a lot of crime happened in the park so it was much feared, especially after dark. The council decided to clear the rubbish, clean out the lake, make new plantings everywhere and employ two full-time wardens to patrol it. Now it is very popular; people feel safe amongst others and enjoy the attractive space. It is open from 6 a.m. to 11 p.m. and there are always people about, which in itself gives an added sense of protection.

The Wildlife Trusts run successful wildlife projects, each over a longer period and often working with teenagers, especially in urban areas. Youth Clubs, English Heritage, the RSPB and the National Trust for example offer opportunities for young people and support for schools.

Public spaces and school design

Many councils are exemplary in their provision of green places, and some developers ensure that poorer communities have beautiful spaces. Recreation grounds do well with play equipment dotted about rather than confined to one area.

In some poorly designed school playgrounds, trained staff are 'policemen', shouting and using whistles instead of respecting children's self-esteem and dignity. Some children are very vulnerable on the playground, needing solace and protection. In creative playgrounds staff can be the children's friends. Fear of accidents, insurance restrictions, litigation and health-and-safety requirements restrict freedom of vision in some park and playground design. *'Playground used at own risk'*. What picture does that give children and young people? *'No children allowed'*—*Take care on swings'*—'No cycles'—'No climbing'—'Steep incline'—'No ball games'*. These messages also mean *'No fun'*. Naturally children should not be allowed to do everything. Respect for both people and the environment is important, yet when there is nothing to fear and privacy is not infringed, why not allow the children to play? Are some young people not learning to take responsibility for their actions because they are warned so much? Beautiful old trees have been felled because of their leaves on the pavement in autumn. Yet slippery leaves were safe enough for thousands of years. How are you supposed to feed the ducks when the village pond has been filled in? It is my conviction that if recreational spaces are designed with joy, play, challenge and movement in mind, apprehension and dread will be transformed into warm sensibility and trust, so unpleasant things are less likely to happen. If teachers make risk assessments, have professional safety checks on equipment, follow official procedures and take sensible precautions, there is no need for alarm. Schools report a positive effect where outdoor design is considered important. I have had the same impression for over 40 years. There is a move to put more emphasis on the outdoors in teacher training and refresher courses. In Appendix 1 I have written about fulfilling government learning objectives beneath the sky. The Play England organization is helping schools acquire a new attitude to risk, something like: 'Accidents will happen anyway, so we are going to allow this-and-that level of risk because the benefits of this-and-that activity are so great that they outweigh the risk of an accident.'

Children with a disability seek out their own activities just like other children. In a London school for the blind the children have a great time swinging high, doing archery and even other things many able-bodied children are not allowed to do. They build up their independence and self-confidence. Their garden was specially designed to allow them freedom and joy.

Forest or woodland kindergartens and schools

The forest kindergarten movement began in Denmark half a century ago. Now not only pre-schools but also schools both on the Continent and in Great Britain spend regular time away from the classroom. Some kindergartens even have no building, others just a shelter somewhere. A hundred years ago, Margaret McMillan established 'shelters' in the city for young children—rather than 'classrooms'.

The teacher of a Swiss state forest kindergarten in the snow, sheltered by a tarpaulin, spoke about the things one can scarcely do outside. 'You have to let some things go: it depends what you think important.' In fact, there is little you cannot do outside. Observation in permanent forest kindergartens is

Our forest kindergarten

Another forest kindergarten

that children are stronger, healthier and more harmonious. In my last years of teaching, my class was outside for about half the week overall. I actually liked to have a balance between indoors and outdoors for the children, to give them different degrees and qualities of protection.

Some 'forest' or 'woodland' schools are a centre for several preschool settings and schools which visit in turn. Children can enjoy forest days or whole weeks, an excellent addition to their curriculum. They are not necessarily in the woods—just in a good outdoor space. The name 'forest' has stuck, but the *idea* can be used anywhere, even in a playground or local park. This is important because many schools otherwise have to use transport. Simply a corner of a playing field or rough space will evolve through devoted efforts. These spaces do not have to be large, just big enough for the number of children to run and climb freely. Spaces are bigger to a child than an adult, as we may remember when looking back. Children bring their experiences

32 Christmas rose

33 Winter-flowering, scented wych hazel

34 Late winter, Camellia

35 Butterfly in Spring

36 Scents, colours, beauty

37 Roses scrambling up lilac tree

38 Hydrangeas have magical shapes

39 Willowherb seeds

40 Compost and leaf mould

41 Farm walk, happy sow with piglets

42 Hungry robin

43 Secret path

44 Autumn fire

45 Nina gardening

46 Colours in public space, bluebells in Royal Botanical Gardens, Kew, at Wakehurst Place

47 More colours in public space, Royal Botanical Gardens, Kew, at Wakehurst Place

home and want their parents to provide ropes, camp-cooking and nest-boxes. Parents enjoy times together outside and like to visit, so it is really helpful if this can be arranged—be it in the garden or woods. I found parents wonderful even when it rained, never complaining in front of the children, or perhaps finding it such fun they did not need to. Rena said that in her kindergarten if it does not stop raining they hang up the tarpaulin shelter, but most children do not bother to shelter underneath it.

As continuity is vital, times in the forest school are best if regular rather than the occasional trip. After an exciting May week in the woods for some combined pre-school classes, the children wanted to carry on but sadly had to wait another year. 'Sure Start', a government programme supporting poorer children and families, funds various projects including some forest centres, especially valuable in deprived areas. Enlightened people work with disadvantaged teenage groups in woods or fields. Not every practitioner is familiar with the outdoors, so training is essential. Reports from woodland schools tell of enhanced self-confidence, courage and independence, and better social and physical skills. Children seem to be friendlier with more concentration, stamina and spatial awareness. Hands-on learning leads to improved physical, literacy and numeracy skills. From my early teaching days, I have spent a lot of time out-of-doors with various classes and ages. We used to cadge lifts on tractor-trailers and watch forest-rangers' enormous fires, but such spontaneous excursions are restricted today by health-and-safety rules.

In the forest school or kindergarten, children are never short of playthings. They soon have handfuls of leaves, sticks, cones and twigs—providing food for the imagination and stimulating love of the natural world and each other.

In summary

What can you do in an imaginatively created garden or playground or such an 'educational' forest setting? Everything I have written about in this book! Play, sing, whittle sticks, chat, climb, dig, make dens and nest-boxes. You can build, listen, run, watch small creatures, count tree rings and listen to stories. Making puppet plays, learning woodwork, cooking, eating and drinking or investigating the forms of bark are just as effective outdoors as in. Under the sky is the place for proper clothing and foot-wear, quiet conversations and making a noise, for being together and alone. For many children today, school playgrounds and woodland kindergartens or schools are almost the only places they are outdoors. They enjoy the peace and food for body, soul and spirit they imbibe there. So let us make sure they have such spaces to enjoy, whether in the forest, big garden, recreation centre, marsh or backyard.

10

Case Studies: Garden, Kindergarten and School

Over 40 years, I have built up four gardens from mainly grass or scrub: first two family ones, then the kindergarten at the same time as the garden in our present home. It is marvellous and life-enhancing to be surrounded by nature, however modest. The first garden grew within an orchard. The second was in a scrubby, sandy area near the sea; eventually it became quite productive. The third we transformed from a dull, grassy housing estate garden. For 13 years of these garden projects I was a lone parent; but my children have helped so much, not only at home but also in kindergarten where parents, assistants and friends did too. I have always been very sad to leave a garden I have made, but that is life: someone else can enjoy it! I will briefly describe the one we have now.

OUR OWN GARDEN

On moving 21 years ago, we discussed what to do with the excess paving slabs around the house and garden, and the soggy and sloping lawn at the back. We decided on a pond below with retaining wall halfway up. We cut and rolled 8-inch-thick turf from the upper part. The boys, aged 12, 14 and 16 had fun smashing up many excess slabs with a sledgehammer. Such physical and tiring activity is fitting entertainment for the gangly, rapidly changing young person! We used the slabs to build a curved, stepped containing wall across the lawn, with concave semicircle of old brick steps in the centre: lovely for thyme, chats, reading (and kindergarten picnics!). We dug a pond, using the earth to fill in behind the wall. My eldest son, who spent spare time on a farm, brought a tractor load of soil to add to the infill, which we carted through the narrow passage to the back in what seemed like hundreds of barrow loads. We then replaced the turf. Now the lawn was on two levels, good to lie on, play volleyball and other games, easy to mow and interesting to look at. We made narrow flower and herb beds along the top of

OUR GARDEN PLAN

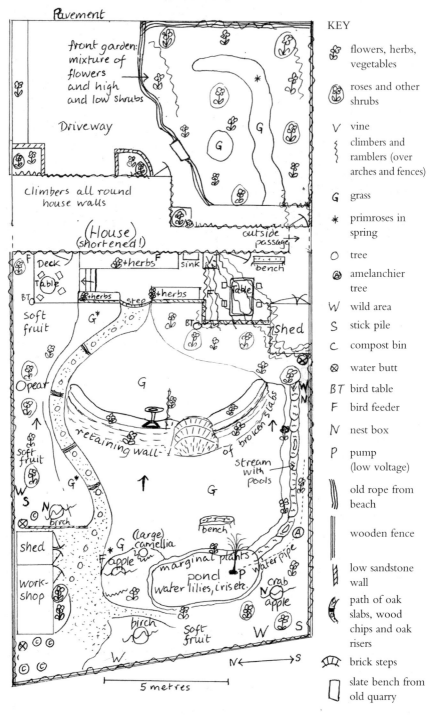

KEY

§ flowers, herbs, vegetables

© roses and other shrubs

V vine

{ climbers and ramblers (over arches and fences)

G grass

* primroses in spring

O tree

© amelanchier tree

W wild area

S stick pile

C compost bin

⊗ water butt

BT bird table

F bird feeder

N nest box

P pump (low voltage)

old rope from beach

wooden fence

low sandstone wall

path of oak slabs, wood chips and oak risers

brick steps

slate bench from old quarry

Retaining wall of smashed slabs

the wall, and planted flowers, vegetables and herbs where the slabs had been, all around the house and perimeter of the back garden. The pond gradually filled with rainwater, to which we added a bucketful from an existing one to encourage small pond creatures, then water lilies and other water plants. Imagine my joy on coming home from a weekend conference to find the children had built me a stream with little pools running down the side of the garden into the pond. An old washing machine pump drew water from the pond up to the top. Later, we added a simple fountain to help aerate the water, a low voltage pump and a bench. It is still a focal point of the garden. The kindergarten children loved it when they came regularly as a class, and still do when they visit now I have 'retired'.

We built a cycle shed, and the remaining slabs and concrete drive were often decorated with oily rags and bits of bikes! Nowadays my husband and I have folding bicycles which fit into a little space, so the shed houses garden things. After the old garden shed disintegrated, we built a new one which also became a workshop. Before that, the children used to push the car out of the garage and use this for their handiwork. They have their own homes now, and we exchange planting, growing and nature tips. They are wonderfully helpful and adept in practical ways, from rebuilding my kitchen to plumbing the garden sink.

Over the first few years we planted two birch trees from seedlings from the last garden, fruit trees and bushes, roses, climbers and shrubs, both to provide

Winding path

beauty all year round but also homes for wildlife. We enjoy a small variety of soft fruits and vegetables in our small garden.

In the front garden, one of the boys made foot-high walls by the house for beds sitting on the concrete which could not be dug up. Being so shallow, they need extra water in dry periods. We added movement all over the garden by giving beds and paths interesting shapes and putting up pergolas of chestnut branches for a vine and climbing plants. For about eight months of the year we mostly eat outdoors, often beneath the vine, even on a sunny winter day. A parasol serves in sun and rain.

The front garden was just lawn, so we gradually replaced it with plants, higgledy-piggledy in beds of curving shapes. We have no edible things there as it is next to the road. Children enjoy playing on this quietish road.

OUR KINDERGARTEN

This is in the Sussex Weald, part of a Steiner Waldorf School. When I came, there were beautiful trees—a hazel, a horse chestnut and two turkey oaks—and rather far away there were swings and an enormous playhouse. The children climbed in a macracarpa hedge and willow tree, next to a flower bed and (muddy) slope up to a lovely big sandpit. The huge grassy area was kept cut by a tractor. There was no fence to most of it so we had to keep an eye out that no one ran away. I believed that making the garden more interesting and embracing would help prevent this. Many of the photos in this book were taken there.

First we bought benches for parents to sit outside while waiting, then gave the sandpit a cosy feeling with a flower border. Next, we divided up the grassy space with large shrub and vegetable beds and compost heaps. We planted two apple trees and old roses from a parent's garden. We begged branches and logs for play. The space became more intimate. But rabbits came in their hundreds to enjoy what we struggled to grow, even onions. So I begged for a rabbit fence: 1 metre-high wire netting dug into the ground 15 cm downwards and 15 cm outwards. Gates and a stile allowed us beyond the garden. (Nowadays one would not be allowed such an unfenced setting.) We grew roses and hedgerow plants along the fence. I rarely bought anything; most was from my or friends' gardens, or roots and cuttings. We made a fireplace of old bricks, and a maypole hole. Every autumn we planted more bulbs everywhere and extended the flower beds next to the classroom. My sons built steps up the muddy slope. One of them dismantled the playhouse (naturally after discussion), and used the materials to make a little house much nearer with his brother and cousin. A friend built two bridges to it (photo in chapter 5) and we made several other paths of different materials, partly to deal with the extensive winter mud, some of which resulted from molehills. Earth from various projects made a bank and hill.

Kindergarten steps

OUR KINDERGARTEN

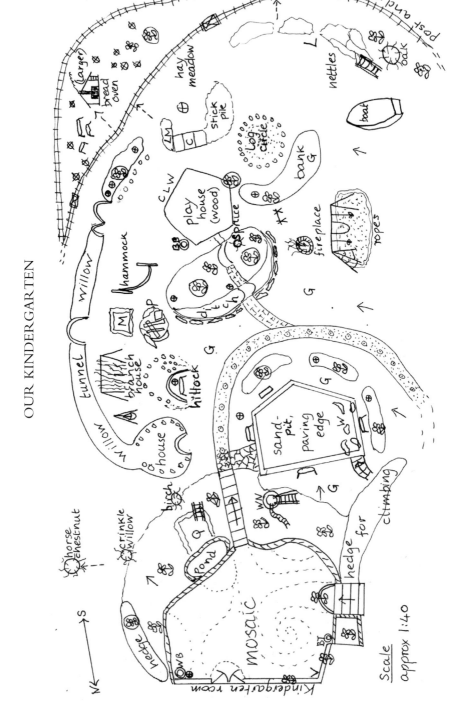

KEY FOR OUR KINDERGARTEN

🐝	herbs/flowers/vegetable	🗔	box for sand tools (gardening tools kept indoors)
🌸	flowering shrubs/roses		
⊕	fruit/nut/berry tree	🅐	'kitchen' (suspended bucket)
✗	other small tree	⋆⋆	sawing horse
G	grass (and molehills!)	⋒	archway
C	compost	⌐	bench
LM	leaf mould	BT	bird table
WN	woven willow tree 'nest'	BB	bird bath
V	vine	♀	quarry
WB	water butt	⣿	wood chips
o	logs on end, some long	∪/⌒	bridges
☉	slice of oak branch	▨	crazy paving
w	pieces of wood	▦	brick path
L	large pieces of branch and tree (for scrambling about)	⊞	wall (low) brick or sandstone
		M	mud pit
P	planks etc. for Treasure Island	▦	steps (up)
CLW	cart, ladders, wheelbarrows	↗	slope up
▱	ladder	--↗	further away
◈	rope ladder		

Next came a willow house and tunnel, then a mosaic with tiny decorated pond. There had been sharp stones outside the room, which needed much weeding and hurt the children if they fell, so a mosaic terrace seemed the answer. It took two weeks of daily work, but was worth every sweated moment. We all had so much fun: assistants, my own and kindergarten children and kindergarten families. The children made pictures in trays, and enjoyed helping in various ways, watching the concrete mixer and carting materials about. Later we put up swing ropes near the little house, made a mud pit and the children dug a 'quarry'.

A few years before I retired, our bread oven took shape on the concrete foundation of the original playhouse, through the kindness of colleagues and 15-year-old pupils. It was one of the best things we did—the whole of Friday

Scrubbing the muddy swinging bridge

mornings revolved around it all year. It is still in regular use. See photograph in chapter 6, p. 109.

We were unable to have animals because of the difficulty of looking after them out-of-hours in that rather isolated place. But there were many grey squirrels (unfortunately no red ones), insects and birds to watch; sometimes a cat or baby fox would appear, even a robin in the room. Cows or sheep with their young grazed in the field behind the fence; they got out occasionally and caused excitement. Deer nibbled the fruit trees and slugs chewed beans and other luscious plants. There was occasional vandalism but we cleaned up and carried on.

It makes me breathless to remember the effort over all those years, for it *was* effort. Yet my determination, support from many kind people and the joy of the children enabled those visions to become reality. Parents and friends enjoyed the garden too. We returned after one half-term to find the parents had made three wonderful benches by the sandpit, all in secret. They did many splendid clandestine things, tear-jerking and heart-warming, right to the end of my time there. In my experience, parents have much love for their children and teachers, even if the going is sometimes tough. I am deeply grateful for their commitment.

ALBEMARLE PRIMARY SCHOOL

In 2006 I was invited to propose alterations to the Albemarle Primary School playground in Wimbledon, London. I emphasized that this project would take time to realize, and ideas would change as it matured. It should become a wonderful place to work and play, expanding and enhancing the curriculum.

The school is single-stream, years 1 to 6, with the 3 Rs: 'Resourceful, Resilient, Responsible'. They won 'Highly Commended' as a 'green' primary school in 2007. The head teacher, Laurie-Ann Lamb, and a parent, Grainne Warner, are enthusiastic leaders of the playground committee. After two visits I drew up plans, which were amateur as I have not trained in landscape architecture, but the aim of this book is to inspire you to do things yourself. Those illustrated are condensed versions. On my third visit, my landscape architect son Mark accompanied me as I needed his professional expertise. Plans are being gradually realized as this book is in preparation. Latest developments are marked in italics.

Situation, topography, climate

The school is in a leafy, hilly area with park, common and lake. The playground enjoys mature trees and varying contours, creating areas flowing into each other. The climate is relatively mild, the soil sandy. Solar panels with meters create interest. Most of the children in this multi-ethnic community walk to school. They signed the 'Walk to School' Charter in 2007.

Initial concerns and enthusiasm

Some parents at the school were keen for change while others were nervous about safety and money. Anxiety and worry from parents about hygiene, water, fire, sand, mud, heights and other risks was a hurdle which received sensitive and knowledgeable handling. Several became enthusiastic and excited, saying, 'Stop talking about it and just get on with it!' Increased understanding of children's needs and learning has helped overcome their fears. The head teacher emphasized that the project is in the children's best interests. 'What if a branch falls down?' asked someone regarding swings and ropes from trees, but she reassured them: there is an annual inspection and all branches are sound.

The school is struggling against a 'forbidden' health-and-safety culture, while promoting opportunities for the children. Activities which have not previously been allowed due to safety or discipline concerns are changing. For instance, children now look forward to playing behind certain bushes. Clambering up a mound with boulders used to be forbidden, whereas it has become a most popular place for play. Going down dips to the fence and jumping off (low) walls: these formerly forbidden activities are being given new life. Many children had until recently seen themselves in a 'prohibited' culture of safety rules. For example, when asked about swings and ropes, they, *the children*, said it would not be allowed. I saw examples of this on my first visit, such as a child trying to climb a slope, whilst another said, 'You're not allowed up there.' A girl was standing on a 16-inch high wall, but others told her to get down, explaining to me this was in case she fell off. Now the school is at pains to change the risk-averse culture within our society to one of 'safely risky' adventures which allow the children to flourish in body and soul.

Help

I suggested Saturday workdays for adults and children with a barbeque or bring-and-share lunch. The venture was discussed at parents' meetings. Lists of needs and work could be decorated and placed where everyone can see them, with spaces for names or initials, encouraging others to add theirs. Each class might take on a modest project. School parents, relations and friends have many amateur and professional skills: builders, artists and other crafts-people amongst them. Initially reluctant parents and teachers often begin to enjoy being involved. Interest might snowball when fuelled by the children's excitement. Parents offered to dig and plant, do carpentry, bring big branches and logs. Some playground staff were really interested and keen to work differently. I advised the school to contact Groundwork, the London Wildlife Trust and/or Learning Through Landscapes. *They joined Learning Through Landscapes in autumn 2006.*

Funds

Money had been gathered through grants and the school budget. At present, 'The Environment' is the planning theme for funding. In future one could propose 'The Arts' for mosaics, 'Drama' for an amphitheatre or 'Creative

Activity' for play opportunities. My idea of 'Wildlife' for the back garden cannot now take place as it is to be built on to become a community centre. It is important to demonstrate that the children are involved in the venture, as well as growing, weeding, watering, compost preparation and leaf-sweeping. They can grow flowers, including bulbs and winter-flowering plants, for classrooms and offices. Groups of children could take turns to cut and arrange them. *In January 2007 a grant of £10,000 was awarded for resurfacing the new multi-purpose area.*

Observations, conclusions and objectives on my initial visit

I observed playground activity, from which I drew conclusions and for-mulated ideas for further supporting children in physical, social, creative and intellectual skills whilst increasing independence, self-confidence and self-esteem. These are combined below, not listed separately as I gave the school. I have not recorded ages because most activities and ideas are spread across the range. Further below are more detailed suggestions under 'Plans'. In order not to weary the reader with repetition, I have not included most of the finer points here which I gave the school, since such details are to be found in preceding chapters.

Equipment and furniture

Children used thin plastic skipping ropes to tie up hoops and themselves to make a train. They needed suitable ropes for tying, and heavier skipping ropes. They had no balls, as these disappear. Playground staff chose the equipment and collected it afterwards. Children might prefer to choose and care for tools and equipment, which would engender trust and responsibility. Wooden sheds and bins would be more attractive than the present plastic ones.

Activity

Many children played noisy football, dominating the playground. Some were happy to do so, some from peer pressure, others from the lack of other focus. I believed the urge to play football would diminish with more variety on offer. *This has been borne out.*

The main path ran along the end of the pitch; with the absence of netting,

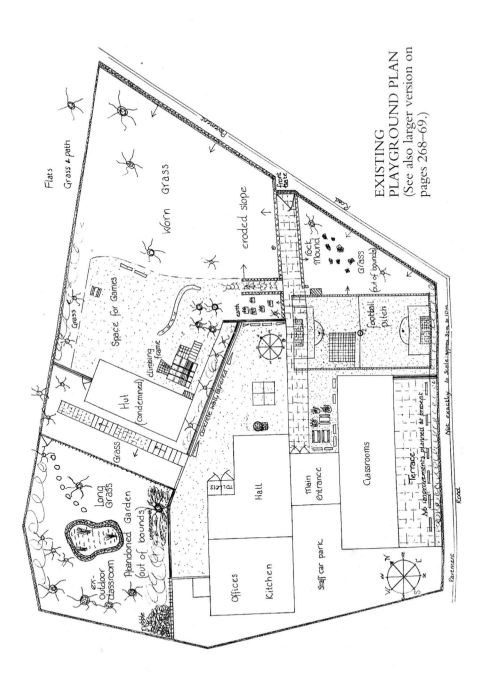

EXISTING
PLAYGROUND PLAN
(See also larger version on
pages 268–69.)

Flats

Grass & path

Worn Grass

eroded slope

Pavement

Space for Games

climbing frame

Hut
(condemned)

Grass

Long Grass

Abandoned Garden
(out of bounds)

ex-
outdoor
classroom

rubble

Offices

Kitchen

Hall

Toilets

Main
entrance

Staff car park

Classrooms

Terrace

No improvements planned at present

Not exactly to scale: approx 1cm to 10m

Road

concrete wall tapered

earth

football
pitch

rock
mound

Grass
(out of bounds)

front gate

Pavement   Road

KEY TO EXISTING PLAYGROUND PLAN

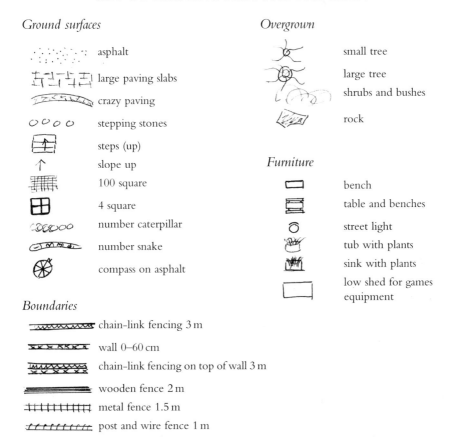

Ground surfaces

asphalt

large paving slabs

crazy paving

stepping stones

steps (up)

slope up

100 square

4 square

number caterpillar

number snake

compass on asphalt

Boundaries

chain-link fencing 3 m

wall 0–60 cm

chain-link fencing on top of wall 3 m

wooden fence 2 m

metal fence 1.5 m

post and wire fence 1 m

Overgrown

small tree

large tree

shrubs and bushes

rock

Furniture

bench

table and benches

street light

tub with plants

sink with plants

low shed for games equipment

people were often hit by the ball. Staff, including playground staff, told me they disliked football; there was constant trouble, aggression and arguments and children got hurt. They thought children and parents would rebel if it were stopped. Children trying to play netball were intimidated by the football frequently flying into their spot. Many were racing aimlessly and noisily around the playground. Others were standing about shyly, at a loose end. Some were lying on the tarmac, becoming rough; several were getting stones out of the earth with twigs. I thought the antisocial behaviour in the toilets would probably be replaced by the creative activities which were going to become increasingly available through the school's new policies.

Playground staff were chatting with children, giving instructions and blowing whistles. Eventually, whistles might not be necessary in a new playground culture. They played a game with a dozen children. They could introduce more ball and skipping games, supporting language, physical, numeracy and music development. Many children were on the climbing frame, whilst boys were trying to slide down, dig and scramble up eroded slopes. Some talked to me excitedly about what they would like. By offering a wider range of fulfilling activity to suit all temperaments and characters, I believed aimless running and shouting would be channelled. Interest, initiative and involvement would be initiated through more creative focal points. Digging and unsupervised play with building equipment would invite imagination and sociability while furthering large and small motor skills. All playground activity can be included in planning and assessments. (See Appendix 1.)

Girls and boys gathered round a mother, cooing and wanting to hold her baby. They would enjoy somewhere sheltered, domestic and quiet for privacy, secrets and being (apparently) unobserved. The children were mainly friendly and obedient; they obviously wanted to fulfil their need for movement. They cannot escape, and observant staff would know where they were. Enticing places and corners could be created, leading to imaginative, constructive, social play, conversation, storytelling and drama.

Albemarle School, present front entrance

Future social space with planting and seating

Mound before rock removal with potential amphitheatre

Original football pitch

Design for the school

Whole area

The trees, contours, natural divisions, rocks and wildlife garden are inspiring. One can envisage non-specific areas within one whole, each allowing several different activities. Paths, hedges, steps and walls would give a sense of flow and freedom. Children attach themselves to objects, so would benefit from more planting and equipment. Climbing plants would soften the chain-link fencing, attract wildlife and render it impossible for people to pass things through from the street.

Paths: Varied surfaces with plants and seating would invite movement, imagination and games. A curving hard-surface path to the top area is needed so children in wheelchairs can go up too.

Steps: *Uneven, irregular ones winding up the rock mound were made in summer 2007 by Graìnne's husband.*

Sheds: Wooden ones for equipment and tools.

Safety surfaces: Sand and wood chip contained in log borders. Recycled tyre surface is obtainable in warm colours.

Seating: Along walls, within trellis or willow fencing, or free-standing.

Wildlife: Build a fallen stick pile under the trees. More nest boxes and feeders. New shrubs for nesting areas.

Plantings: Make flower, herb and vegetable beds of varied heights on trellises or wires along walls in curved or zigzag raised beds. Remove tarmac, fill in with compost. A 3-metre space between beds on the long concrete wall would encourage ball games, especially with a tile pattern or picture. Sinks by the sloping path could be used elsewhere if a stream is built there.

Plant bushes providing flowers and berries for birds and butterflies in the dip by the road fence. *This was done in summer 2007. Also a pack of hedgerow plants was acquired from a newspaper offer.*

Build a shaped wall of trellis with plants and seating above the proposed terraced area. Construct a small playhouse with turf roof. Plant a willow tunnel and/or house along the top outer fence.

The school could grow extra vegetables in a council allotment for lunches.

Front entrance area—social meeting point

This would present an integrated social element. New ground surfaces, seating and additional plants in tubs or holes in the ground will break up the area, making it welcoming and interesting. Social interaction and con-versation would be encouraged whilst offering protection for reserved children. Outdoor furniture and plant pots naturally check random ball playing, confining it to designated places. Skipping can take place here. Gràinne suggested spirals of benches. Like a maze, it would satisfy the chil-dren's love of going in and out, exploring and getting lost. Existing bench and table corners could be rounded off with a jigsaw until replaced by freely designed seating. Light needs to enter windows and classes need privacy, so seating must be at a distance. A sawmill has been contacted about shelters. The tall street lights could be re-painted and have small trees planted alongside. There might be a grant for solar-powered ones.

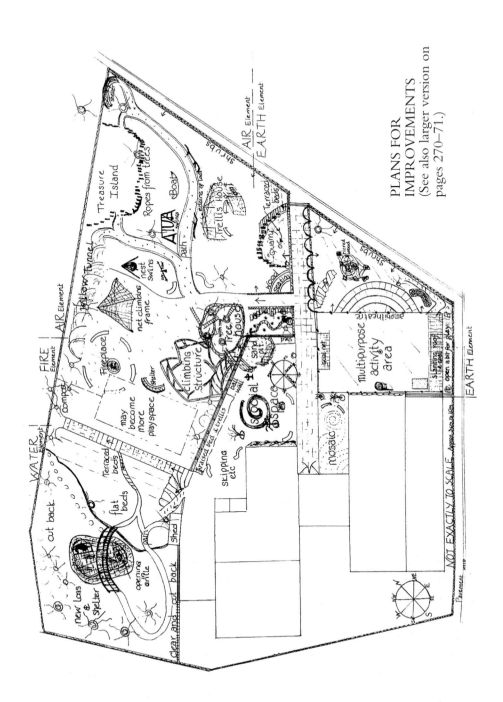

PLANS FOR
IMPROVEMENTS
(See also larger version on
pages 270–71.)

KEY FOR PLANS FOR IMPROVEMENTS

Ground surfaces

synthetic sand-filled carpet

sand for safety surface
(or red asphalt, partially
rubberized)

light, multi-coloured paving
(as large existing path)

wood chip

sandpit for long and high jump

gentle slope for wheelchairs,
lower gradient to airy element
area than at present

stream with solar-powered
pump

pool and fountain,
solar-powered

mosaic with shelter,
seating and plantings

Furniture

various shapes of seating

low playhouse

large spiral seating

sundial

Boundaries

soft netting

cricket netting with
removable poles

logs set into ground

branch on ground

arches for climbing plants

wooden railing 1 m

peepholes in wooden
fence

trellis with plants

Mosaic: This would be so eye-catching. Classes could make individual parts for a large one. Children and parents would enjoy finding pieces for it.

Long wall: Plants supported by wires (on the diagonal to discourage climbing). Parallel gutters running down the sloping end could invite rolling ball/leaf/pebble/water play, using short ladders. A sundial would be interesting.

Sunken sandpit: The whereabouts of possible underground pipes must be uncovered before construction. Six square metres would be a practical size. The existing roughly 60-degree corner would lend itself to a polygonal pit. Plantings up trellises all around with a 'doorway' about 1.5 metres wide would slow down running in and out and give summer shade. Sand would be easy to contain within such a boundary. Small rocks and logs within the sandpit would provide a contrasting texture.

A shed for sand equipment could have hooks for waterproof trousers in different sizes for wet weather, to allow as much sensory outdoor experience as possible all year round. Autumn leaves can be raked out. Hooks and eyes could secure a tarpaulin cover.

Lower area—focus: earth element

Rock mound: Owing to safety concerns (some rocks were 1 metre high and had jagged edges) this was out of bounds on my first three visits. All the rocks are geologically interesting. I had suggested the bigger ones could be surrounded by slatted wood to three-quarters of their height for sitting, climbing and jumping off, or moved into a circle with wooden bridges and a grotto underneath. The boulders' flatter tops would allow sitting and standing as a look-out. Wood chips or sand would be an appropriate safety surface. Mark suggested taking the largest one, 1 metre high, to the new social area, surrounding some of it with plants which would stop climbing whilst displaying its interesting contours. The other two large ones could be placed at each end of the proposed amphitheatre, framing the 'auditorium' and making a solid part of the construction.

During Autumn 2006, a small bulldozer was engaged to move the rocks apart and sink the bigger ones half into the ground, so that the children could play on them and so use the mound. The largest was put near the front gate where the children are not allowed anyway, and the other big ones were put where the amphitheatre could be. It was done while the children were present, as I had suggested, stimulating excitement, adventure and science. One day a decorative windmill could adorn the top.

Amphitheatre: Built into the mound, the all-purpose pitch would be the stage. Brick, stone, paving, or soil and turf with wooden risers could make steps. Upright poles driven close together into the ground with boards behind would contain turf. Plays need not necessarily take place on sunny middays (the auditorium would face south) and baseball caps would suffice. The amphitheatre would suit plays, gymnastic displays, dances and concerts.

Football pitch, becoming multi-purpose games area: Netball, volleyball, football, races, group ball games and long-rope skipping could take place here. A centre hole could accommodate a maypole. Long and high jumps along the wall towards the road with sandpit at the end would be fun. No markings would be necessary; children could just take whatever space they needed to run. Chalk and tape measure could mark lengths when wanted. Two holes would contain the removable upright poles, hooked to the wall when not in use. These jumps would make for hands-on maths.

Removable aluminium poles and cricket netting could replace chain-link fencing and open up the area. A slanting upper end by the road would stop balls going over, as they do at present. *In spring 2007, the space behind the football pitch was opened up and replanted for play. In summer 2007 new green fencing sheltered the main path and opposite end of the pitch, while a low wooden wall built along part of the mound side caught stray balls. Much of the perimeter fence has been covered with willow matting.*

Sand-filled synthetic-grass carpet could be laid. The children wished for grass, but with so many children it would wear out and become muddy. It will be decided which markings are needed for which games. Probably one could manage with few. The 100 square will not be redrawn. Football really only needs centre and penalty spots and D markings, which latter could be drawn as a circle and so used for other games. *The sand-filled carpet was laid in summer 2007, also over the mound and steps as the grass was wearing out. Now even the parents enjoy the mound and steps for sitting and chatting.*

Foot and hand-holds on a curving wooden structure against the wall would create a climbing challenge and more interesting façade.

Front gate

Garden: Terraced beds would look attractive and show people what the children are doing. First I suggested compost heaps and leaf mould along the back fence (proper compost doesn't smell). Mark said it would be better to have them nearer so they are more accessible and integrated. They could be behind the terraces by the road. New planting everywhere will need compost.

Walls: How could these be freed for climbing, jumping and walking? They could potentially offer movement and exercise, and an opportunity for risk and challenge—really not dangerous. A lower step alongside them might be an answer, except one might trip on the step . . .

Top area

Focus: airy element

The children's wish for climbing and monkey bars would be met by ropes, swings, trapezes, rope ladders, see-saw, large hammock, roomy climbing structure and tree house. Bridges curving up and down could cross a path or shallow ditch. A washing line with basket of pegs would be nice for the younger children, either just for play or for real washing they had done. Ropes, also with pulleys, could be attached to trees or from posts on the slope to the front path. *Long ropes, one a long loop and the others with knots at the bottom, were hung from the trees in 2007. The children were overjoyed.* There would still be room for running around but the 'buildings' would contain aimless racing about.

A tree house built between the four trees on the corner would be superb. Short ladders would lead into it. It would be safe surrounded by wooden railings with sand underneath. *(See chapter 5 for my design for the tree house here.)* Younger children would also enjoy a low playhouse. A structure of 2–4 upright posts with 1–2 poles across the top, which could allow making ever

New ropes

Happiness on the new ropes

new dens with loose branches, poles, planks and string, would suit all ages. See under *Houses* in chapter 5 about such dens that can be frequently rebuilt.

Every other board could be removed from the wooden fence, creating a look-out over the lower playground. Shapes could be cut but would require shoring up behind. Eventually something lighter and slightly lower could replace it.

The climbing frame is not entirely safe and needs replacing, perhaps by something more spacious. *It was closed off in spring 2007.* I showed pictures of wooden and rope equipment to the committee. Big branches connected to each other (adhering to safety rules) would be lovely. Apparently one can

Beautiful old trees for big tree house

take dead wood from the common, so children could take the 20-minute walk to collect branches to lie on the ground. This would help them to feel ownership of the space, besides which the carrying would be sociable and stretch physical skills. It could be part of a PE lesson. A parent and van could collect larger branches. Because of concern about children running off, one might need to choose them carefully. On the other hand, children respond to challenges, adventures and one's trust, and enjoy well-earned praise. Large log slices (even a yard wide) can often be obtained from councils which have to fell trees. They can be put on top of each other safely. The local authority can check them.

For a 'Treasure Island', a boundary of horizontal logs held in place by pegs would prevent things rolling downhill (except where it could be allowed). Ideally it would be a minimum of 25 square metres, and uneven in form to provide more creative opportunity. The perimeter fence could be a part of the border. Staff would ensure string and rope are not mis-used. *By autumn 2006, various pieces of wood were acquired which children were really enjoying. Even the biggest boys and girls used leaves, sticks and stones to dec-orate.* The children could have a 'quarry' in the eroded area near the front gate if not used for planting, or next to the 'Treasure Island'. The fact that the front slopes are eroded shows the children's need for scrambling, dig-ging and sliding.

Holes in the asphalt for trees or bushes would divide up the space, making it more interesting whilst leaving room for ball or other games. A natural surface would be more environmentally and children friendly.

Focus: fiery element

A fire-pit could be made beyond the trees using old bricks. With risk assessments and strict rules it would be a fine learning resource and enjoyable for parents on workdays too. Children could gather sticks for it. Perhaps eventually a bread oven could be built.

Focus: watery element

A shallow stream with a liner or waterproof cement next to the sloping path to the top area would be beautiful, incorporating water plants, descending pools and fountain. A pump would circulate the water. Existing sinks could be kept. The school could fundraise for a flowform, with a science slant to a grant request.

An old wooden boat might be acquired from a Thames rowing club (to put on the ground!). It might have a mast, and there could be old cloths and string available to make sails. It would be used by many children for endless 'river' or 'seaside' play. Oars could be used if the children learn to take care with them.

Several water butts were on order when I first visited the school, excellent for the new gardens. A bird bath or two would also attract children.

With growing water shortages, it would be useful and beautiful to have a turf garden on the flat school roof eventually. Along with plantings and water butts, this would absorb water otherwise going down the drain. It could be created with prepared rollout wild flower matting and simply used for wildlife if the roof does not support much human weight. Reinforced and with adequate fencing, what miraculous plantings and fruitful lessons could take place up there! What about a grey water system one day . . .

Wildlife garden—focus: also watery element

2008: A Community Centre building is now planned over this wildlife garden, but I record my ideas for my favourite place in the school, as readers might be inspired to make use of a similar neglected area.

Children could rediscover this beautiful space with its lovely trees, pretty bushes and pond. A membrane under rubbish, brambles and logs shows it was once an outdoor classroom. Stepping stones hide under overgrown grass. The sloes and rose hips could be picked and made into syrup and jam. The spruce and birch would be beautiful covered with little lights at a Divali or Christmas festival at the end of the school day. I am convinced there would be room for the whole school to squeeze in and sing together!

Many primary schools enjoy a pond. This one needs clearing of duckweed which cuts out light so limits life below. A safety grille just under the surface with opening parts for pond-dipping and decorated with flat metal forms such as a frog or dragonfly could be funded by an arts or wildlife grant. The low water level was the same in autumn and summer despite rain, indicating that the liner leaks. If safety issues cannot be overcome, it could be filled with soil to make a bog garden.

Old wildlife garden

Achievements and the future of the school

Having visited several times at the time of writing, I am delighted to see the progress. The children have some better surfaces for play. The new work has brought about a change in their activity. Football no longer dominates. The mound swarms with children who play, climb, have adventures, roll and slide.

The head teacher told me that soon after it was opened up with its randomly cut steps and imagination-inspiring wooden fence at the top, a boy came rushing up, flung his arms round her and said, 'Got to go, I'm playing pirates...!' Teachers say the new multi-purpose area has completely transformed the playground and the children's behaviour—they just love it. The sports teacher says he now has the facilities to teach sport properly. The long ropes are very popular. The hut will be replaced by an eco-building, with a £100,000 interest-free loan and potential council funding to match it. It may be moved back to free more space for play.

As this is an on-going project, I can only describe its beginning. But it is wonderful to share in bringing more joy, movement and creativity to these children.

Albemarle School, new green mound with new screens, wall and fences

New multi-purpose green games area with new fencing

In summary

It is wonderful for parents, friends, staff and children to create something inspirational and lovely together. So if you are part of an early years' setting or school and have not yet expanded your outdoor provision, have a go! The rewards in terms of children's physical and imaginative development are incalculable.

CONCLUSION

Nature and the cosmos are majestic and vast, far exceeding humanity's wisdom or intellect. Nature can be surprising, terrifying, joyful or mysterious. The earth and its wildlife belong to all humanity equally, but they are not our possessions. It is vital to understand our interdependency with the natural world; and in recognition of this many people today are actively protecting and promoting cultural, social and bio-diversity. Our own survival and that of the planet depends on children developing love and respect for the natural world and learning to act as its committed custodians.

I am convinced that children who grow up to love and wonder at the beauty of nature will care for its treasures with heart and spirit, concern and determination. I believe the best way to grasp humanity's impact on the planet is by experiencing nature first-hand. Enabling children to be active outdoors kindles love and respect for nature, thereby encouraging altruistic responsibility in them when they grow to adulthood. True freedom, its roots in a wholesome childhood, is selfless, not egotistic. I cannot emphasize enough how children's outlook is influenced in a positive way beneath the sky and stars. Healthy development of body, soul and spirit needs freedom to grow in simple, unpressurized, healthy environments. The innocence of childhood is universal; the same needs live in rich and poor alike. Yet the forces of capitalism, competition and egotism are very strong.

I heard a young man chatting with a very old lady. 'We're going to York to see the train exhibition with the children. It's quite a long way, about 300 miles and several hours' drive but it's worth it as the children will love the exhibition.' She wondered aloud whether they might not prefer a more local trip to a historic railway.

> 'Machinery that gives abundance has left us in want.' Charles Chaplin, in the film *The Great Dictator* (1940).

This visionary statement dates from quite a long time back. Since my childhood there has been an explosion in the use of gas and oil: fossil, unrenewable energy. Many think there is no time for working by hand any more, yet machinery needs time, money and energy to produce and maintain. Simple things reduce dependence on oil and eliminate harmful emissions, increase our good health and give a fine example to the young, such as raking instead of leaf blowing, walking or cycling to school and taking up shears instead of a hedge trimmer. Using less water and catching it in butts reduces the need for new reservoirs or extracting water from rivers. Producing conventional fertilizers is energy-intensive but returning to the soil what came from it (the natural fertilizer) is a basic premise of organic agriculture. Children can learn to value such principles in work and play outdoors. Re-duce, re-use, re-store, re-make, re-pair, re-cycle, equal re-spect: these are the principles of permaculture and ecological, sustainability which alone can safeguard our children's futures.

> 'Organic three gallons petrol, please,' said a child playing garages. Wouldn't it be nice?

'Urban agriculture' and 'transition towns'—those aiming to become carbon-neutral through sustainability and diversity, inspired by Rob Hopkins (see Appendix 2)—are new concepts to help our ailing planet. Architects are incorporating recycled materials, effective insulation, solar panels, windmills, 'grey water' diverter systems and water butts into their 'eco-build' designs. Local, seasonal organic or biodynamic food, animal-friendly farming and farmers' markets reduce energy use. Is it not friendlier to take children to a small shop rather than a vast supermarket? Many children do not watch their parents gardening or help with cooking, so it is really wonderful if they get involved in these activities in their setting or school. The 'Food for Life Partnership' gives children opportunities to visit farms and grow and cook their own food. Schools are increasingly using unprocessed and organic fare. Our local biodynamic farm has the motto 'The future is our responsibility'.

People have inspiring ideas for our children's future in combating global warming and climate change: how to prepare for a post-fossil-fuel age and engage in 'energy descent' (using less). The children growing up today may have real survival questions to face. Yet if they have developed devotion and wonder for the natural world in childhood, and deep respect for the way others think and feel, they will be stronger to cope with problems, and more likely to extend generosity towards poorer nations. If these chapters have inspired you to develop or begin to make lovely gardens and playgrounds

Sven picking lime blossom

with open-ended possibilities for children, you will give them inestimable inner strength. Some children have too much homework, which keeps them indoors, aside from the time they spend with electro-visual and -aural media. I have been told there are successful classes for children with challenging behaviour who do not go inside at all (but have been unable to find out where). That must be an incentive for others to let the children out too!

A parent said her son, now 10, had had so much fun in our outdoor activities, and he wouldn't have been the same without this. She felt it opened up parents' perspectives on being outside. I have much for which to be grateful to parents, who sometimes struggled to understand and come towards me in our outdoor activities. My knowledge, experience and joy gained in the open air throughout childhood and young adulthood stood me in good stead for my teaching and parenthood. My own children absorbed from babyhood the wonderful world outside. They slept under the sky during the day, picked lime flowers for tea infusions and blackberries for jam, played amongst gorse bushes and bracken and built 'factories' with old slates and bricks. Birthday parties were sometimes in a boat of pebbles and sand on the beach, on a rock in a stream or round a campfire. As they grew, they took on an increasing responsibility for how they treat their environment, extending their love of the natural world into responsible action and guardianship. (See also Plate 45: Nina gardening.) One of my children said recently, 'Appreciation of nature is more important than tangible things,' and another, 'I'm a child of nature. We all are.'

Children find joys of nature close to home: shiny beetles, wide horizons, flowers pushing out of asphalt, willowherb opening its petals on burnt ground and magnificent purple thistles growing on rubbish dumps.

'Mummy, the moon is broken ... (pause) ... Never mind, Granny will mend it.'

Lars in his organic field

Mark

Sven chopping for the stove

Sven (R) and friend on the way up

Healing forces surround us outdoors. There is wonder in the heavens, music in birdsong, falling water and chirping crickets. A child laughed: 'The leaves are clapping their hands!' Nature's colours bring a breath of fresh air. Beauty surrounds children in little flower, big tree or dragonfly. Movements of sun and

Child of nature, now grown up

stars, waxing and waning of the moon, growth and dying of the seasons, flowers opening and fading and fruit ripening: these are comforting rhythms for children. They experience warmth in exercise, sunshine and love for each other and the world. All such phenomena bring healing to body and soul.

Traffic park of the future . . . ?

Children given a wide range of opportunities for movement will also develop mobility of brain and warmth of heart, so vital for working and cooperating with others. They find infinitesimal secrets if we have the heart, eyes and ears to leave them free—free to take child-appropriate risks and to play imaginatively with nature's playthings in all seasons outdoors. They appreciate unhurried time: time to be joyful, to play, eat, sleep and grow; and time to be brave and to understand, to be peaceful with loved ones. Untidy back streets, woods and open spaces hide a myriad of self-development and bravery-building opportunities. Let us take courage to let children play there, under the sky. As adults we often need to be brave in tricky and stressful circumstances; the more such courage matures in the child, the better. In fear, adrenalin runs faster, helping us meet a challenge with greater courage. In extreme fatigue, we often get second wind. I hope this book has inspired the reader to take courage and find new directions in living, celebrating and working with children.

One of my sons said: 'Nature is my god. My church is here, outside.'

APPENDIX 1
THE EARLY YEARS FRAMEWORK

The 'Every Child Matters' UK government framework for all children emphasizes the importance of wholeness of development, embracing four principles: 'A Unique Child; Positive Relationships; Enabling Environments; Learning and Development'. This is all realizable outdoors for all ages of childhood. The 'Early Years Foundation Stage' ('EYFS') is embedded in this framework. Everything I have written in this book has an element of working with all of the 'EYFS' outdoors, as they all overlap and flow into other areas. For example, 'Observe fascinating phenomena such as ... the way leaves and feathers descend zig-zag or twizzling through the air at different paces, or catching snowflakes and seeing them through a magnifying glass' (area 4). These involve mathematical theories (area 3), underlie physical skills in trying to catch them while falling (area 5), stimulate the imagination (area 6) and language (area 2) whilst invoking joy (area 1).

Young children develop towards future thought processes, IT work and mathematical understanding through playing freely and imaginatively with the multi-faceted playthings and equipment which nature provides, thereby enhancing large but also small motor skills which support literacy and dexterity of mind. The following is a sample of possibilities. Children, with their enthusiasm and initiative, appreciate our being flexible, so are happy if we are willing to abandon our plans when the occasion warrants it.

Education is most effective when not confined to little boxes.

Personal, social and emotional development (area 1)

Find joy, reverence and wonder, creating the basis for future sociability.

Express needs, wishes, joy, sadness and other feelings.

Have respect for the garden or other play space, which in turn grows into respect for each other.

Show reverence and respect through sharing tools and equipment and tidying away afterwards.

Children of all cultures play, walk and work happily together with their unspoiled universal awareness.

Serve food to others rather than oneself first.

Learn to cope with not having the wanted tool or not being wanted in others' play.

Share and take turns with tools, barrows, other apparatus and space such as sandpit, playhouse, climbing structure, swings.

Learn how to react to each other's moods and needs.

Enjoy being alone in a quiet corner of the outdoor space.

Care for someone who is sad to be alone.

Work and play in groups or alone.

Build structures such as houses and dens, strengthening feelings of security and identity.

Older children help younger with such things as dressing, sandcastles, climbing and on walks.

Younger ones gaze in wonder at the abilities of older children.

Grow in courage to walk through long grass/brambles/in the rain, etc.

Watch and imitate adults, e.g. builders and those working with the children.

Play with and without structures and equipment. (Under the age of 6 children need physical things to play with; older children may just want the space.)

Collect left-over crumbs for birds, feed and water them.

Care for pets, farm animals, tools, sandpit and pond.

Learn about safety relating to tools, fire and water.

Gain independence in dressing, walking distances, getting out and putting away equipment.

Maypole dancing.

Communication, language and literacy (area 2)

Talk and negotiate together in pairs or groups.

Talk to pets and other animals.

Explain objectives, difficulties and situations to each other.

Ask adults and each other for help and advice.

Listen to and understand explanations and suggestions, e.g. how to cross a fallen log, sow seeds or make a castle for balls to roll down in the sand.

Listen to stories told outside.

Learn vocabulary through imitation and repetition in conversation, stories and ring times outside.

Use verbs in describing activities.

Use nouns in describing objects.

Use adjectives in relating experiences.

Sing together and alone.

Organize and make up games and activity together, using speech and body language.

Play games such as Grandmother's Footsteps and Fox and Chickens.

Develop balance and coordination through climbing, scrambling, digging, jumping, sowing, watering, skipping and walking in wind or wading in water.

Develop dexterity as a pre-writing skill through such things as sowing seeds, weeding, playing in sand and mud and with small natural materials.

Make pictures and books about activities.

Draw attractive, colourful plant labels.

Problem-solving, reasoning and numeracy (area 3)

Use mathematical language through hands-on activity and real experience, achieving early concepts:

Number, e.g. 'Look how many earwigs we found!' Some count them (inaccurately at first). 'Let's put three earwigs back and the rest on the stick pile.' 'Is there room for another child?' 'Let's pick very few daisies.' 'Two spades are missing.' 'Who has no tea yet?' 'How many more spoons do we need?'

One-to-one correspondence, e.g. place one seedling or two seeds into each hole, give one picnic cup to each person, hang up tools in their correct places.

Categorizing, e.g. sort shells/stones/pine cones/balls into their containers; put tools and equipment neatly in rows/on shelves/in containers; put dried herbs into different pots; make patterns with various natural materials; put apparatus and toys away in order of size or shape.

Comparatives and superlatives, e.g. 'My wheelbarrow is heavier than yours.' 'That log is lighter than this fat one.' 'I have less sand than you.' 'We haven't got more water than he has.' 'My twig is thicker than yours.' 'We've made the biggest castle!'

Positioning, e.g. 'My ball is about to fall off the wall.' '... behind the shed/at the end of this path/by the top of the steps/under the board/near the bird bath/below the window sill/at the back of the tool shed'.

Measure and size, e.g. 'How deep is the water/that hole?' (gauging with stick, boots or own body). 'How high is that tree/the sky?'; 'This plank is quite wide.' 'We have to bend really low to creep through this tunnel.' 'How much more compost do we need?' 'The bird bath is nearly empty.' 'Those long logs for the fire go on this pile, but those short, thin ones are only for kindling.' 'How much further do we have to walk?' 'How far is it back to school?' '...a huge sunflower!' '...teeny weeny ants.' Measure, cut, sort and stack wood for a fire or bread oven.

Geometry, e.g. fold cloths and tarpaulin, wind up string into balls; make designs in sand and mud; observe shapes, patterns and forms in nature, for example leaves, caterpillars, frost on blades of grass, changing clouds, winter tree skeletons, the way leaves grow up stalks, spirals in pine cones, arrangements in flower petals; sow seeds in rows, circles or other shapes.

Shape and size, Explore seeds, leaves, bark, petals, trees, stones, etc.

Knowledge and understanding of the world (area 4)

Curiosity is kindled and exploration and discovery are encouraged through play, leading to future awe and understanding of science.

Enjoy holistic activities through the seasons, e.g. for apples: tree pruning, blossom, fruit, windfalls, picking, crumble, juicing, putting bits with worms onto compost heap so they can continue eating.

Observe, for instance, insects, bees, butterflies, rabbits, clouds and moon.

Play with 'toys' from the natural world.

Building with or watching adults: what is needed, how it is put together, how the tools are sharpened and cared for.

See newborn lambs, calves, kittens, piglets, etc. (or being born).

See young animals growing into adult size, shape and character.

Learn about the elements—

Earth/mineral:

Observe snowflakes and frost through magnifying glass.

See texture changes to sand and earth in different weathers.

Observe and handle stones and crystals.

Make and use compost and leaf mould.

Experience slowly evolving phenomenon of new soil in compost.

Water/plants:

Watering; what is enough or too little?

Collect rainwater in butt/buckets.

Measure precipitation in bucket or bird bath.

Sail boats, especially in moving water.

Observe transformation of tadpoles, newts, toads, dragonfly larvae, caterpillars.

Pond-dipping.

Grow and prepare food.

Squeeze fruit or vegetable juice in a press.

Cut and dry herbs.

Observe plant growth and metamorphosis.

Plant willow or hazel for houses, etc.

See and experience qualities of plants: healing, stinging, prickly, tall, short, touch-me-not, etc.

Observe height and size of seedlings for pricking out.

See how well plants grow without weeds, with compost and enough water.

Find out why, when plants do not thrive.

Make physical plant protection from slugs, birds, moles and deer.

Air:

Feel wind directions; see where prevailing wind is by tree growth.

Watch trees in wind.

Put on muslin 'fairy wings' and feel the effect in the breeze.

Observe phenomena such as floating leaves and feathers descending zig-zag or twizzling through the air at different paces.

Make parachutes and kites to show what wind (moving air) does.

Bird watching, including migration.

Feed and water birds, make nest boxes.

Warmth:

Encounter compass points in the movement of the sun (and sometimes moon during the day).

Experience light and shadow, heat and cold.

Feel wind, hot sand or ice on the skin.

Prepare wood for fire.

Light, kindle and tend a fire or bread oven.

Put on sun hats and lotion, dress warmly in the cold and put waterproof gear on in the wet.

Wear appropriate footwear.

Care for animals, birds, worms, etc.

Experience love of other children, adults and the natural world.

Physical development (area 5)

Expand large motor skills:

Use of buckets, ropes, pulleys, gardening and sandpit tools, carts, wheelbarrows, logs, branches, balls and hoops; roll, swim, swing, jump, slide; cope with slippery surfaces; cross a fixed or swinging bridge, balance on plank; jump and wade in water; walk up and down steps; jump off walls, logs, steps; climb tree, bush or hedge; build in play; turn and sieve compost; move to beds and smooth out; plant larger items (bushes, trees, hedges); help with creation of playground or garden; help adults, e.g. building paths, beds, playhouse, stream, bridge, steps, or hedge laying; maypole dancing.

Expand small motor skills:

Sandpit and mud play; patterns in sand or earth with fingers or small tools; play and decorate with small natural objects; gather and prepare vegetables, berries and fruits; knead bread; pick and arrange flowers; sow seeds; prick out seedlings; wash dolls' clothes and bedding; peg out washing; wash and dry up.

Creative development (area 6)

Enhancement of imaginative, inspirational and artistic sensitivity:

Play freely, including decorating and making puppet plays with natural materials:
flowers, bark, berries, conkers, shells, pebbles, crystals, rose hips, nuts, grasses...

Create houses with pieces of wood, cloth, string, branches...

Play in 'Treasure Island' and willow or hazel structures.

Use all areas, also the roots of a tree, or rocks.

Use changing textures through weathers in sand and earth: frozen, sticky, dry, wet,
soft, hard.

Encounter textures, colours and forms, including changes through the seasons.

Listen to birds, water, animals, wind, rain.

Smell different scents in flowers and all sorts of gifts of nature.

Make and taste jam, syrup, soup, crumble, etc. from own-grown and wild-collected
food.

Enjoy songs and verses in 'ring-time'; sing bird songs, copy animal sounds.

Listen to and tell stories.

Artistic, craft activities: draw and paint; make frost paintings; use plants for dyeing;
make bark rubbings and lavender bags; press flowers and leaves for transparencies:
arrange flowers; make moving pictures.

Maypole dancing.

Adults share ideas, design and build new areas with children, e.g. paths, beds, playhouse, mosaics.

Use growing imagination to deal with tricky social situations and solve problems.

APPENDIX 2
FURTHER READING, RESOURCES, INFORMATION, GLOSSARY

Further Reading

I have not listed any nature guides: what pleases me may not be what you need. You can find books on birds, nests, eggs and nestlings, mammals, reptiles, insects, fish, pond life, sea life, fungi, trees, wild flowers (which generally includes grasses, shrubs and possibly trees). Below is a small selection of books to do with the outdoors:

Berger, Susan, *Allotment Gardening, an Organic Guide for Beginners*, Green Books, 2005

Brickell, Christopher (chief editor), *Royal Horticultural Society Encyclopaedia of Gardening*, Dorling Kindersley, 1992

Cooper, Stephanie, Fynes-Clinton, Christine and Rowling, Marije, *The Children's Year*, Hawthorn Press, 1986

Druitt, Ann, Fynes-Clinton, Christine, Rowling, Marije, *All Year Round*, Hawthorn Press, 1998

Druitt, Ann, Fynes-Clinton, Christine, Rowling, Marije, *The Birthday Book*, Hawthorn Press, 2004

Edgington, Margaret, *The Great Outdoors*, Early Education, 2002

Goddard Blythe, Sally, *The Well Balanced Child*, Hawthorn Press, 2004

Goddard Blythe, Sally, *What Babies and Children Really Need*, Hawthorn Press, 2008

Hillier, Malcolm, *Garlands*, Dorling Kindersley, 1992

Howarth, Maggie, *The Art of Pebble Mosaics*, Search Press, 1994

Jenkinson, Sally, *The Genius of Play*, Hawthorn Press, 2001

Lockie, Beatrys, *Gardening with Young Children*, Hawthorn Press, 2007

Mabey, Richard, *Food for Free*, Fontana Collins, 1972

Meade Faulkner, John, *Moonfleet*, Penguin Pop Classics, 1994 (originally 1898)

Mellon, Nancy, *Storytelling with Children*, Hawthorn Press, 2000

Moss, Stephen, *Bird-Friendly Garden*, Harper Collins, 2004

Mullan, Clare, *Light Reflections (poems)*, Leiston Press, 2006

Oldfield, Lynne, *Free to Learn*, Hawthorn Press, 2001

Opie, Iona and Peter, *Children's Games in Street and Playground*, Vols. 1 and 2, Floris Books, 2008

Organic guides, *Green Essentials* (a series endorsed by the Soil Association and the Henry Doubleday Research Association), Impact Publishing, 2005

Ouvry, Marjorie, *Exercising Muscles and Minds*, National Children's Bureau, 2003

Packham, Chris, *Back Garden Nature Reserve*, County Wildlife Trusts, New Holland, 2001

Pearson, David, *Treehouses*, Powell's Books, 2001

Rae-Smith, William, *A Guide to Water Gardening*, Bracken Books, 1989

Readman, Jo, *Controlling Weeds Without Using Chemicals*, HDRA/Search Press, 2000

Robinson, Peter, *Water and Rock Gardening*, Hermes House, 2003

Royal Horticultural Society, *Simple Steps to Success* series, Dorling Kindersley, 2007

Schweizer, Sally, *Well, I Wonder, Childhood in the Modern World*, Sophia Books, 2006

Seymour, John, *The Complete Book of Self Sufficiency*, Faber and Faber, 1975

Sigman, Aric, *Remotely Controlled*, The Random House Group, 2005

Steiner, Rudolf, ed. Matthew Barton, Festival Series: *Easter*; *Whitsun*; *St John's*; *Michaelmas*; *Christmas*, Sophia Books, 2007

Steiner, Rudolf, *The Kingdom of Childhood*, Rudolf Steiner Press, 1982

Tait, Malcolm, ed., Royal Horticultural Society (RSC) and Wildlife Trusts, *Wildlife Gardening for Everyone*, Think Books, 2006

Warnes, Jon, *Living Willow Sculpture*, Search Press, 2001

Whitefield, Patrick, *The Earth Care Manual*, Permanent Publications, 2006

Wilkes, John, *Flowforms, The Rhythmic Power of Water*, Floris Books, 2003

DVDs

Pickup, Steve, *Making Living Willow Sculptures,* Permanent Publications

Jonathan Steddall, producer; *Time to Learn*, 110 minutes; 1992; a survey of Steiner Waldorf Education, in which the outdoors and my kindergarten play a part.

Steiner Waldorf Schools Fellowship, available in PAL or VHS
www.steinerwaldorf.org.uk

Resources and Information

Clothing

Apart from shops:
Hip sling seat www.smilechild.co.uk

Outdoor clothing:
Muddy Puddles *www.jccountry.co.uk*
Raindrops *www.raindrops.co.uk*

TOGZ *www.togz.uk.com*
www.waterproofworld.co.uk

Underclothing:
BORN, organic, also prams *www.borndirect.com*
Greenfibres, organic/biodynamic *www.greenfibres.com*
Muladula *www.muladula.com*
Natural Clothing, organic *www.naturalclothing.co.uk*
Patra, silk *www.patra.com*
The Baby Gift Place, organic *www.thebabygiftplace.co.uk*

Compost

Peat-free organic compost: look locally first, including local authorities which sell
   compost. Vermiculture (worm compost) *www.wigglywigglers.co.uk* or
   www.wormsdirect.co.uk

Craft equipment

Mercurius *www.art-makes-sense.com*
Myriad *www.myriadonline.co.uk*

Cycling

Environmental Transport Association *www.eta.co.uk*
CTC, UK cyclists' organization *www.ctc.org.uk*
National Cycle Network *www.sustrans.org.uk*
North Sea Cycle Network *www.northsea-cycle.com*
Sustrans, sustainable transport *www.sustrans.org.uk*

Education and support outdoors

BBC's Improvement of 50,000 local sites *www.bbc.co.uk/breathingplaces*
Creative Partnership; organization for educational projects
   www.creative-partnership.com
Eco Schools *www.eco-schools.org.uk*
Free Play Network/Risk Assessment Workshops *www.freeplaynetwork.org.uk*
Friends of the Earth: also teaching resources *www.foe.co.uk./learning/educators*
Groundwork UK *www.groundwork.co.uk*
Hiram Trust, also bread ovens *www.hiramtrust.org.uk*
Learning Through Landscapes *www.learningthroughlandscapes.com*

National School Grounds Week *www.ltl.org.uk*

Organic Gardening for Schools *www.gardenorganic.org.uk/schools_organic_network*

Outward Bound Trust *www.outwardbound.org.uk*

Play England *www.playengland.org.uk*

Play Scotland *www.playscotland.org*

Play Wales, Chwarae Cymru, *www.wales.org.uk*

Playlink *www.playlink.org.uk*

Real World Learning *www.field-studies-council.org/campaigns*

Rethinking Childhood *www.rethinkingchildhood.com*

RISC; environmental educational projects including edible landscapes
www.sector39.co.uk/risc

RSPB junior section: Wildlife Explorers *www.rspb.org.uk*

Ruskin Mill: young people with learning disabilities' workshops
www.ruskin-mill.org.uk

Safe Routes to Schools *www.saferoutestoschools.org.uk*

Scouts and Guides *www.scouts.org.uk*

Steiner Waldorf Schools Fellowship *www.steinerwaldorf.org*

Sustainable development in school communities *www.suschool.org.uk*

Sustainable environmental design *www.gaiaeducation.org*

Walking bus *www.foe.co.uk/learning/educators*

Wildlife Trusts' junior section: Watch Groups *www.wildlifetrusts.org.uk*

Youth Matters *www.dfes.gov.uk/publications/youth www.cat.org.uk*

Environment, energy and water savings, sustainability and climate change

See also Education, Food etc.

Campaign for Dark Skies *www.britastro.org/dark-skies*

Living Lightly on the Earth, Positive News *www.positivenews.org.uk*

Friends of the Earth *www.foe.co.uk*

Permaculture *www.permaculture.co.uk*

www.climatechaos.com

www.climatecrisis.net

www.foe.co.uk/living

www.forumforthefuture.org.uk

www.greenbuildingstore.co.uk

www.nef.org.uk/energyadvice/co2calculator.htm

www.rainharvesting.co.uk

www.rspb.org.uk/green www.rspb.org.uk/climate

www.stopclimatechaos.org

www.suschool.org.uk

www.thecarbontrust.co.uk
www.transitiontowns.org

First aid kit of natural remedies

Weleda *www.weleda.co.uk*

Food, Gardening, Composting and Farming

Promoting healthier food, protecting children from junk food advertising
www.sustainweb.org
Slow Food; defends small retailers and regional traditions *www.slowfood.com*

Organic:
Biodynamic Agricultural Association *www.biodynamic.org.uk*
Demeter *www.demeter.net*
Food For Life Partnership *www.soilassociation/foodforlife.org*
Garden Organic (working name for the Henry Doubleday Research Organization)
www.gardenorganic.org.uk
Permaculture *www.permaculture.co.uk*
Soil Association *www.soilassociation.org* and *www.whyorganic.org*

Fruit presses

www.harrodhorticultural.com
Vigo Limited *www.vigoltd.com*

Funding

Awards for All *www.awardsforall.org.uk*
Eco Schools *www.eco-schools.org.uk*
New Opportunities Fund *www.nof.org.uk*
Suschool awards *www.suschool.org.uk*

Grain mills and grinders

www.hehlis-holistics.com

Places and reserves to visit in the UK (Please see local information in other countries)

Many individual places are on maps and advertised locally.

Centre for Alternative Technology, Machynlleth, Powys, Wales SY20 9AZ
www.cat.org.uk

County Wildlife Trusts *www.wildlifetrusts.org.uk*. Each county has its own trust and
   website.
English Heritage *www.englishheritage.org.uk*
Natural England: Local and National Nature Reserves, Greenspaces (towns), Sites of
   Special Scientific Interest, Special Areas of Conservation *www.naturalengland.org.uk*
Farms open to the public: check local advertisements.
National Trust *www.nationaltrust.org.uk*
Ramblers Association *www.ramblers.org.uk*
Royal Botanic Gardens, Kew, Surrey, and at Wakehurst Place, Sussex *www.kew.org*
RSPB (Royal Society for the Protection of Birds) *www.rspb.org.uk*
Woodland Trust *www.woodland-trust.org.uk*

Playground equipment

Using untreated timber from sustainable sources:
www.kompan.com
www.thechildrensplayground.com
www.timberplay.co.uk
Rope structures www.corocord.com

Protection of childhood and children

Alliance for Childhood: international forum, fights poverty and neglect, promotes
   better health, strengthens family life, protects children from commercial pressure
   and counters children's dependence on electronic media
   www.allianceforchildhood.org
The Children's Society *www.thechildrenssociety.org.uk*

Reclamation of building materials and recycling

Besides locally:
www.freecycle.org
www.salvo.co.uk
www.wrap.org.uk

Tools, barrows, carts, accessories

Try locally; ask your local blacksmith. Some crafts people remake adult tools into children's. Try
lighter ones made for women. Also:
www.art-makes-sense.com

www.bramblecorner.com
www.harrodhorticultural.com
www.magiccabin.com
www.permaculture.co.uk
www.thecountrygardener.co.uk

Turf

www.turf.co.uk
Sand-filled synthetic carpet: amongst others *www.nottsport.co.uk*

Willow

www.essexwillow.co.uk
www.willow1.fsbusiness.co.uk
www.thewillowbank.com
www.sector39.co.uk
www.geocities.com/willowpool
www.westwaleswillows.co.uk

Wood

Forest Stewardship Council *www.fsc-uk.info*

Poisons in nature

Wild and common garden plants

Many plants in Britain are poisonous, though only a few are dangerously so. In many only part of the plant may cause discomfort. Some poisonous plants are also used in medicine or as a herb, for example *Atropa belladonna*, foxglove and rue. The following list is not comprehensive and does not include house plants.

English name	Latin name
Autumn crocus	*Colchicum autumnale*
Black bryony	*Tamus communis*
Black nightshade	*Solanum nigrum*
Bluebell	*Hyacinthoides non-scripta*
Cherry laurel	*Prunus laurocerasus*
Cuckoo pint, lords and ladies	*Arum maculatum*
Daffodil, narcissus	*Narcissus* species
Daphne species	*Daphne mezereum* and *D. laureola*

Deadly nightshade	*Atropa belladonna*
Fool's parsley	*Aethusa cynapium*
Foxglove	*Digitalis purpurea*
Giant hogweed	*Heracleum mantegazzianum*
(rash if affected skin exposed to sun)	
Holly (berries)	*Ilex aquifolium*
Horse chestnut	*Aesculus hippocastanum*
(bitter, so children won't eat much)	
Ivy (bitter, so children won't eat much)	*Hedera helix*
Laburnum, golden rain	*Laburnum anagyroides*
Larkspur	*Delphinium* species
Lily of the valley	*Convallaria majalis*
Lupin	*Lupinus* species
Mistletoe	*Viscum album*
Monkshood	*Aconitum napellus*
Oleander	*Nerium oleander*
Poppy	*Papaver rhoeas*
Potato (when green)	*Solanum tuberosum*
Privet	*Ligustrum vulgare* and *L. ovalifolium*
Rhubarb (leaves)	*Rheum rhaponticum*
Rue (can cause rash if touched skin	*Ruta graveolens*
exposed to sun)	
Snowberry	*Symphoricarpos rivularis*
Spindle	*Euonymus europaeus*
Spurge	*Euphorbia* species
White bryony	*Bryonia dioica*
Woody nightshade	*Solanum dulcamara*
Yew	*Taxus baccata*

NOTE: The castor oil plant (*Ricinus communis*), has *extremely* poisonous seeds (containing ricin). It is a well-known house plant, but is sometimes used in garden bedding schemes.

Mushrooms and berries

Always ask an expert if not absolutely sure.

Snakes

Adders are the only poisonous ones in mainland Britain, recognized by zigzag markings. Bites are rare. There are no snakes in Ireland.

Dead animals

These become toxic, so children should wash their hands thoroughly when they have been handling a dead animal.

Ticks

These can cause serious illness. Higher temperatures are bringing them to Britain. Avoid them by ensuring the skin is covered when walking in long grass or low bushes in summer.

Glossary

Biodynamic/organic: Grown without chemical fertilizers, pesticides or herbicides, in harmony with the environment and protecting animal welfare.

Practitioner: Teacher and any adult who works in a childcare or educational setting

Setting: Place of care and education for young children

Approximate sizes: 1 cm/centimetre is $\frac{2}{5}$ inch; 10 cm/centimetres is 4 inches; 1 metre (100 cm/centimetres) is 39 inches; 10 metres is 133 feet; 1 square metre is 10 square feet

For readers in the USA

Allotment: Small plot of land rented from local council

Biscuit: Cookie

Conker: Nut of horse chestnut tree, large, shiny, brown, wonderful plaything

Goods truck: Box car

Hedgehog: Small spiny animal

Mobile phone: Cell phone

Nappy: Diaper

Netball: Similar to basketball

Noughts and crosses: Tic tac toe

Old banger: Old car

Pants: Underpants

Practitioner: Teacher and any adult who works in a childcare or educational setting

Quoit:	Small ring
Rucksack:	Backpack
Scheme:	Arrangement, plan
Secateurs:	Hand pruners
Sellotape:	Scotch tape
Setting:	Place of education for young children
Single stream:	One class per grade
Traffic calming:	Ways of slowing traffic
Trousers:	Pants
Water boatmen:	Water striders

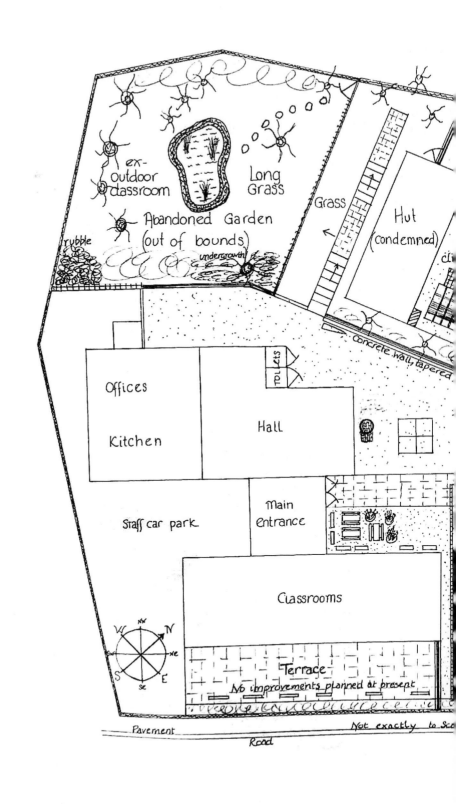

ex-Outdoor classroom

Long Grass

Abandoned Garden (out of bounds)

rubble

undergrowth

Grass

Hut (condemned)

concrete wall tapered

Offices

Kitchen

TOILETS

Hall

Main Entrance

Staff car park

Classrooms

N
NW
NE
W
E
SW
SE
S

Terrace
No improvements planned at present

Not exactly to Sc...

Pavement

Road

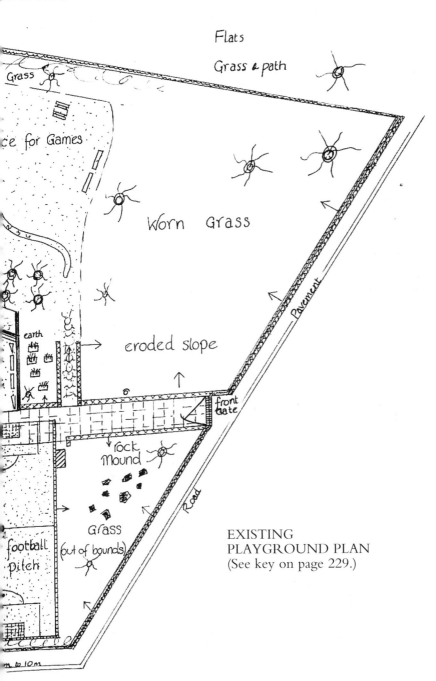

Flats

Grass & path

Grass

ce for Games

Worn Grass

earth

eroded slope

front gate

Pavement

rock mound

Road

Grass (out of bounds)

football pitch

EXISTING
PLAYGROUND PLAN
(See key on page 229.)

m to 10m

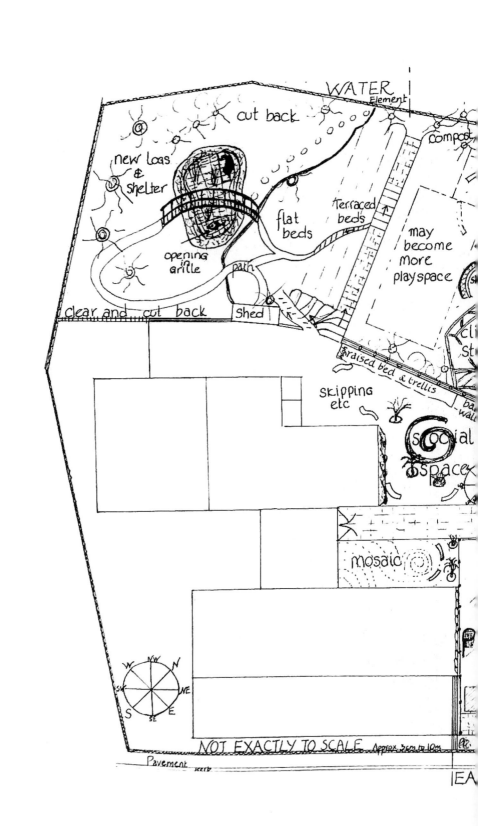

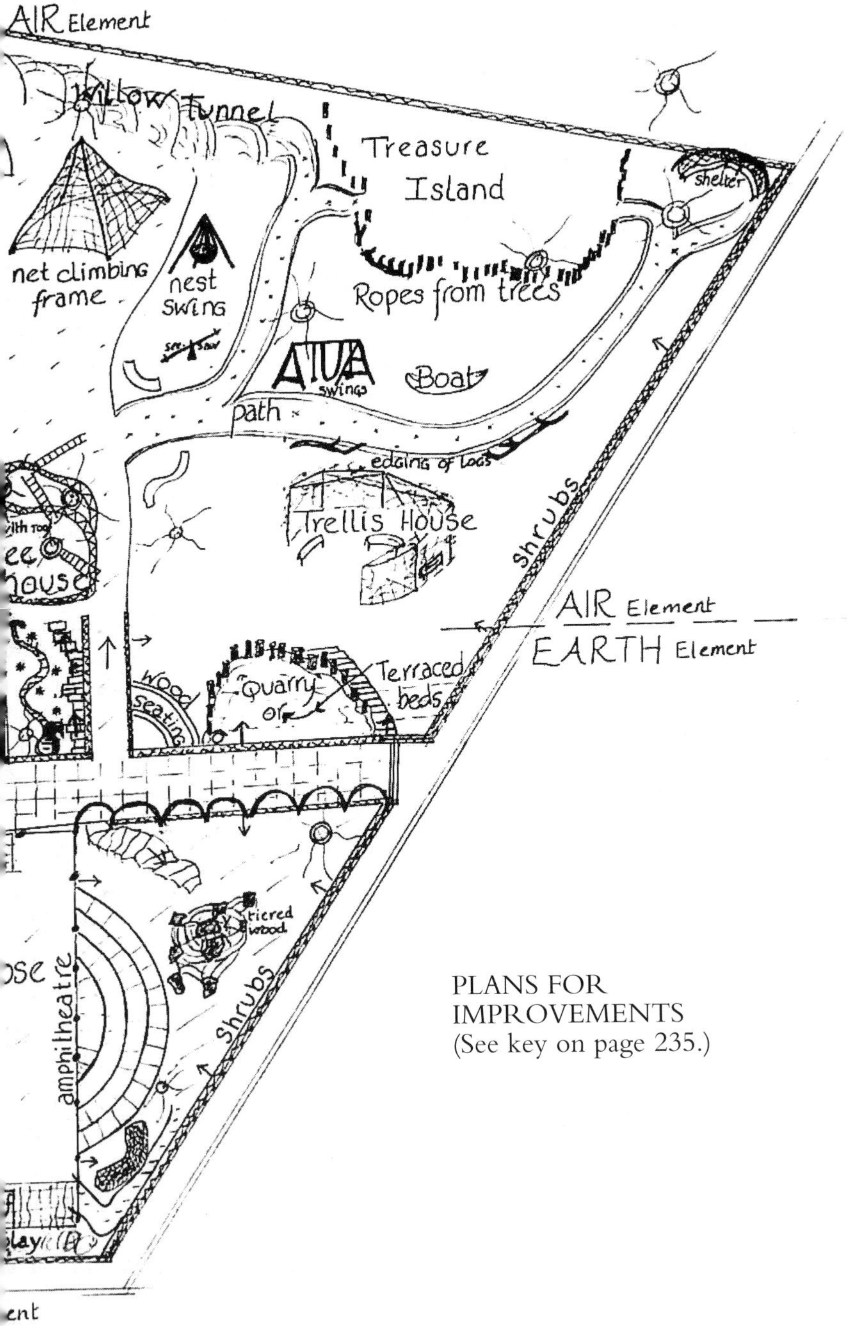

AIR Element

Willow Tunnel

Treasure Island

shelter

net climbing frame

nest swing

see saw

Ropes from trees

ATUA swings

Boat

path

edging of logs

Trellis House

shrubs

with tool

ee house

AIR Element
EARTH Element

wood seating

Quarry Or

Terraced beds

tiered wood

ose

amphitheatre

shrubs

PLANS FOR
IMPROVEMENTS
(See key on page 235.)

lay

ent

INDEX

INDEX OF SONGS